Homeless

Praise for the Book

'Homeless' leaves you wondering whether it is autobiography or fiction, so fluid is the writing, so seemingly effortless the introspection. But by the end of this vital book with its razor-sharp analyses of disability, anomie and sexuality, you don't care. Magnificent.

— JERRY PINTO, author of *The Education of Yuri*, *Murder in Mahim* and *Em and the Big Hoom*

Wry, angry and heartbroken, 'Homeless' is not only an account of growing up lesbian and dyslexic in a dysfunctional family, it is also an evocation of youth itself—the strangely intense mixture of self-confidence and insecurity, of hope and rage that carries us from adolescence into adulthood. K. Vaishali writes with an easy flow and a dry humour to produce an eminently readable memoir.

— PARVATI SHARMA, author of *Jahangir: An Intimate Portrait of a Great Mughal* and *The Story of Babur*

Homeless

Growing Up Lesbian and Dyslexic in India

K. VAISHALI

SIMON & SCHUSTER

London · New York · Sydney · Toronto · New Delhi

YODAPRESS

First published in India by Simon & Schuster India, 2023
and Yoda Press, New Delhi

1 3 5 7 9 10 8 6 4 2

Simon & Schuster India
818, Indraprakash Building,
21, Barakhamba Road,
New Delhi 110001
www.simonandschuster.co.in

Yoda Press
79 Gulmohar Enclave
New Delhi 110049
www.yodapress.co.in

PB ISBN: 978-93-92099-51-9
eBook ISBN: 978-93-92099-50-2

Typeset in India by SŪRYA, New Delhi
Printed and bound in India by Replika Press Pvt. Ltd.

Contents

1. Coming Out

I read online that writing can be therapeutic. I don't know about that, but I can't afford therapy and writing is cheap. I already own a dozen new notebooks that I bought to write novels. Gripping a new notebook now, the prospect of writing fills me with excitement. I have a new idea for a novel and after thinking about it for two hours, I'm convinced that it is going to be the most important novel of my time. But I have seen enough rejections to know that no publisher is eager to publish a writer with a writing disorder when there are perfectly fine writers waiting for a chance to get published. I love the convenience of blaming dyslexia and dysgraphia for my failures—like it's the only way I'm lacking as a writer. Tough industry or not, I have to distract myself. Pretending to write a novel is an effective distraction. Writing in this notebook right now is distracting me from worrying about my situation.

A week ago I had no money, no job, and my rent was due. I rode to the Sabarmati riverfront at five am, wondering if I'd rather die choking on water or the debris of plastic bags floating on the river's surface. What did I have to live for? After searching for a job for months, my flatmate gave me a job in her company as an Office Boy. My responsibilities included walking across the street to the print shop for print outs, arranging logistics, and adding phone balance on employees' phones. It barely covered my rent, and I was laid off in four months. I'm single in a city with eight openly lesbian couples, so low-to-no romantic prospects. My choices were drowning in plastic water, stealing cash, or living on the street—or worse, asking my parents for money.

I got accepted by a Master's programme in Communication at a public university. Packing now to go to University of Hyderabad to live rent-free for two years. I just need to rest my head free of charge—the degree is a bonus. Many of my friends who are in their early 20s like me are struggling to find their place in the job market too. But they get to do that from the comfort of their parents' homes. I can't—I got disowned a year ago after I told my mother I was a lesbian.

Maybe I should tell her I'm not a lesbian anymore and we can go back to pretending to tolerate each other. Because honestly—do I even qualify as a lesbian anymore? I haven't lesbianed in a year. Maybe it's like being a doctor. Once you are a doctor, you remain one no matter how much or how little you practise. Once you've operated, and you've seen the fleshy insides of a human being, you change forever. But I don't remember what holding a woman feels like anymore or how a woman smells. I don't remember anymore how a vagina feels against my face.

I wasn't supposed to write about vaginas on the second page of this notebook. I should have written other nonsense for at least thirty pages before I got to vaginas. Now I have to hide this notebook, or my future roommate in the university will read it and tell the university authorities. I'd be asked to leave the hostel like that other lesbian was at Banaras Hindu University (BHU). There was a news article about it that read: Student asked to leave BHU girls' hostel for 'homosexual' tendencies. They had to use the phrase 'homosexual tendencies'. Couldn't just call her 'homosexual' because that would require actual proof that the authorities don't have and don't need to have to suspend her. Couldn't call it 'lesbian tendencies' as the word lesbian is obscene; so much so that the word—not the act, the word—was censored from the Bollywood film *Dum Laga Ke Haisha*.

At the time of the incident, the Express quoted a professor as saying: 'The tendencies she was showing were at a nascent stage. We cannot really pin-point if it is really homosexuality. But we had to suspend her to maintain peace and discipline in the hostel.' The Express also quoted a fellow student, who did not wish to be named, as saying: 'The student was blind in one eye. She was disabled. The college authorities should have been extra attentive towards her. Instead, they suspended her without an inquiry or counselling. How is she going to face her class now? She has to study with the same women students.'

I wonder how far advanced my 'homosexual tendencies' have progressed. I'm probably back to the nascent stage now. I must dial it back if I have to survive the university and its authorities. I can't get caught having tendencies that dare not speak its name. Must keep this notebook close and guard it. Or tear the vagina pages out.

I wouldn't have come out to my mother if I had known my 'homosexual tendencies' would regress. I had a comfortable life till I came out to her. Got to stay in her comfortable house in Andheri west, had a job showing art house films in an indie theatre, and had a girlfriend. I told my mother about my sexuality and from a wicked curse I lost the house, job, and girlfriend—I lost my Bombay life. Since then, I've been living out of my suitcase, like I am a fugitive on the run.

Which is funny because gay sex was a crime under Section 377 in India when I came out in 2015. I wonder if my life would have turned out differently had my mother called the police to arrest me for having 'unnatural' sex. I would have run away from the police, and moved from city to city, broke, single, and unemployed, doing menial work, which is precisely my life right now. I'd get tired of running and surrender myself to live rent-free in prison, not unlike the public hostel that I'm going to. It would have been better if my mother had snitched on me. At least then I wouldn't have to keep up appearances as her daughter. I wouldn't have to make small talk with her every week about the weather, while she ignored my poor living conditions and my poor diet of a bag of potato chips for lunch and a plate of *dahi puri* for dinner. Jail food would probably be more nutritious.

Coming out was a weird experience. I knew it would be disappointing news to my mother who has been dreaming and hoping since the day I was conceived, that I'd fill the conventional-middle-class-Brahmin-woman shaped mould which she confined herself in. She *just* wanted me to get a degree from a top Engineering college, marry a Brahmin dude and have children, and it would bring her great happiness if I could have *just* done that. But I already disappointed her by not opting for Science in 11th grade. I knew it was pointless to try to compete with others to get into a good engineering college; I knew my intelligence didn't translate to good scores in tests. In a way, I knew I had dyslexia before I knew what dyslexia was.

Then I disappointed her some more by quitting the Chartered Accountancy course and dropping out of my Bachelor's degree. I didn't expect another disappointment to radically change my life. But everything changed the day I came out to my mother, even though I'm not sure if I actually came out to her.

'I like girls,' I declared to my mother.

She tried to make a joke that I don't remember now.

'I am serious, I like girls. I am in love with Bhavya,' I said. 'Do you remember her? We went to see her Bharatanatyam dance performance.'

My mother widened her eyes. She made an angry face and asked, 'Are you pregnant?'

'Are you asking me if I am pregnant?'

'Yeah—'

'How can I be pregnant?' I said, 'You know you need a man to—'

'Did you have pre-marital sex?'

'I don't want to discuss that with you, it's my private life.'

'Did you have pre-marital sex?'

'I won't say.'

'How'd you know if you didn't have pre-marital sex? Answer me! Did you?' She looked raging mad.

'Yes.'

'How dare you have pre-marital sex?!'

'But how can I have post-marital sex with a girl?

How can I marry a person of the same sex? It's not allowed.'

'How long has it been going on?'

'About three years?'

'And you are telling me now? You should have told me earlier so I could have gotten you psychiatric treatment.'

I began an angry rant about how homosexuality is not a mental ailment as she stormed to her bedroom and shut the door. We never spoke about it after that.

I never expected her to respond to my coming out by asking me if I was pregnant. I think her scale for my future had 'married engineer with kids' as the best-case scenario and 'unmarried pregnant college drop-out' as the worst case scenario. My coming out broke her scale, but she was too confused to fathom a scenario worse than an unmarried pregnant college drop-out just yet. I think when she asked me if I was pregnant, she was bargaining with me. It was like she was saying: let's meet in the middle at unmarried pregnant college drop-out, or I walk away.

And walk away, she did.

2015 started with the four of us in Bombay: my parents, my brother, and I. (Bhavya, my then-girlfriend, too, who moved to Ahmedabad in May for her Master's). In February of that year, my father unofficially separated from my mother and moved to Chennai. He explicitly asked her not to come to Chennai after him, to leave him alone. In April, my brother moved to Delhi to study for an undergraduate degree. In June, a week after I came out, my mother, who presumably couldn't breathe the same air as her own perverted pre-marital-sex-having-queer daughter, moved to Chennai to be with my abusive alcoholic father who is guaranteed to call her worthless or physically abuse her if he had had a shitty day.

But it's fine that she moved to Chennai, fair even, since I was using her for my own means. Since I was five, we had an unspoken contract where she'd invest in me and I'd be a 'good daughter' in return. I got food, clothes, and shelter to be obedient and do well in school. When I didn't score 85% or above consistently, she'd tell me in great detail all the pains she was going through to keep her end of the contract down to a single rupee. Every other week she'd say, 'We pay 30 thousand in rent now, increased from 27 thousand last month. Split it by six members, your rent is 5000. Another 5000 in groceries, plus school fees and bus fees—it's all around 10,000 now with inflation. And those pizzas you eat cost at least 2000 a month.'

She was trying to say that the return on her investment in me wasn't higher than inflation. That the money was better invested in nothing.

When I scored well in my 12th grade exams and started studying accountancy, it made her look good. Not engineering-good, but acceptable. We renegotiated and I got a generous monthly allowance, with a special allowance just to buy books. It went to shit when I quit accountancy; since then, she only loosens her purse strings if it is for something respectable.

When I started working in a cinema hall, it wasn't respectable, but we renegotiated the unspoken contract where I'd get food and shelter as redemption for my mother's neglect in not detecting my learning disabilities soon enough. I only got tested at twenty, following a self-diagnosis. She argued her side of the contract well: after all, how could she know about dyslexia when nobody told her about it. But I argued well too: I cited the damage from years of her nitpicking for not doing well in school, for calling me lazy when I was trying so hard. We drew up a new unspoken contract: I'd get food and lodging for a few years till I earned enough to be independent. I deserved a better deal, but I was tired of fighting for myself.

The contract was voided when I announced my sexuality. I didn't think that was grounds for disqualification, but she is no longer negotiating with me. Before she left, she asked me to pay rent for staying in her two-bedroom house in Andheri. The rent was more than my salary at the cinema house. When I asked if I could have roommates, she said no—I guess from the fear that I'd be lesbianing in her house. I realised how impossible it was for me to pay rent and live in Bombay with my prospects. I decided to move out and took the first job I found in Ahmedabad. It made sense since Bhavya was there. Within two weeks, Bhavya broke up with me. And a month later, I was fired from my job. That's how I came to work as an office boy.

I've been going over my coming out to my mother to understand what compelled her to leave. Maybe it's the way I told her I was a lesbian like she'd know what it meant. Maybe she didn't, maybe it was the first time she had heard about homosexuality. Between us, there was no vocabulary to talk about homosexuality after all. I don't know if we even have a word for lesbian or homosexual in Tamil or in other Indian languages. If we did, I've never heard anyone use it. I don't know of any open LGBTQ+ safe spaces, no community centres or gay bars. The only time I've been around LGBTQ+ allies is at Pride marches. Apart from Bhavya, I don't think I know another person with 'homosexual tendencies', and I doubt my mother would have. Maybe she would have reacted better if she had had some context. Maybe if she had some context about the global acceptance around homosexuality, how it is no longer criminalised in many countries, how it is no longer in the Diagnostic and Statistical Manual of Mental Disorders (DSM) manual, she wouldn't have said the thing about 'psychiatric treatment'.

Homosexuality happened to me without much context too. I was 19; Bhavya and I met when we were pursuing a Bachelor's programme in Commerce at Mithibai College. During the winter semester break, we met at Juhu beach every evening to read aloud Virginia Woolf's *To the Lighthouse*. On some days we were the only ones on the beach, lying down on the sand next to each other, hearing the waves roar as Bhavya read Woolf's words, moved to tears. When college started again, we both got busy, and I started reading Leo Tolstoy's *Anna Karenina*. One day, on a silly whim, I messaged Bhavya that we should call our first child Vronsky, a character from *Anna Karenina*. At that point, I had never seriously thought that I liked her or that I liked women or men. I had never thought about having children. It was just a silly whim: probably brought on by the way her breath felt on my back when we rode to the beach on my scooter, or the way I wanted to run my fingers through her hair as she read Woolf.

She replied that she had already decided to name our first child Lily, after a character from *To the Lighthouse*.

After that, we spoke a lot about the house we'd live in, the children we'd have, and how we'd bring them up. It was all a way of flirting but it wasn't so apparent to me then, and it wasn't apparent at all to her. Once we were on a long walk on the road outside Mithibai College, when I felt this intense urge to kiss her. I invited her to the terrace of my building the next day and kissed her cheeks. She kissed me back. I kissed her neck. She twitched, electrified from how much she felt from the kiss.

Finding my sexuality opened me up to the world in a whole new way. Till then, grief was the most intense feeling I had felt, followed by anxiety. But being with Bhavya made me feel such intense passion. It felt like we were the only people in the world—like every day the sun rose from the curl of her lips and got hopelessly tangled in her hair. We were both from broken homes and we cherished and cared for each other with love that we never got growing up. She saw me for who I was despite the forces tearing me down.

For a brief moment, before the world caught on to our love, we were happy.

2. Moving Out

I know I failed miserably in Ahmedabad. I spent a year moping about lost love, drinking bootlegged alcohol that probably gave me stomach ulcers—I'll know the extent of it later if I can ever afford medical attention. I also spent the year searching for employment while surviving on the office boy salary along with a couple of freelance web developer gigs that paid peanuts.

But I try not to take my failure personally. It's not a reflection on my capabilities, although I am not capable at all. I'd probably be struggling even if I were capable. I know this from knowing capable peers who are in jobs much beneath their capabilities. The quandary of underemployment has clipped our dreams. It'll remain that way for a decade at least, the way I see it.

It's common to imagine the job market like tides. A generation of workers rises, hits the shore, and retires. Then another generation of workers rises, hits the shore, and retires. The Indian government's civil service employment is certainly like that, with a few hundred employees retiring every year to make space for the next generation.

But in the Indian private sector, the economic liberalisation of 1992 sent tsunami waves of foreign jobs to India over the next 15 years till 2008. My parents' generation, the Indian Gen X, who were in their twenties and thirties during that time, rode the wave. While the foreign and domestic investment in the private sector grew rapidly, there was a shortage of industry veterans with only a few from the government sector. Many graduates of that time skipped middle management and moved swiftly to senior management in their respective industries. And they probably won't retire till they've bought their fifth house. Gen Xers who were in their 20s to mid-30s in the 1990s will retire when they are 60 in the 2030s.

My generation, the Millennials, graduates of 2008

and later, lost new jobs to the 2008 recession and old jobs to the older generation still holding on to them. All this while the number of job seekers in the labour market grew, with the literacy rate and the percentage of the youth population both higher than they had ever been. So, while the job supply shrank, job demand rose. We have to wait till 2030 at least, till the older generation retires, to be able to find a career ladder and move up. Most of my peers still live with their parents, sending their resumés out interminably, and repeatedly getting ignored.

But my parents don't see it that way. They think they were successful because they were talented, hardworking, and conventional—it had nothing to do with the economy. They have been giving me hell about my career since I turned 18. They want me to achieve corporate success, and they think I can achieve it by appearing conventional. They want me to change; they want me to wear professional clothes, sport a conventional hairstyle, be punctual, get a degree in science with a decent GPA from one of the top colleges, be employed every day of my adult life, have mild hobbies, get married, and have children—just to earn decent money and own multiple houses. They want me to be stable, and they don't want me to be creative.

My parents think I'm struggling to find employment because I ignored their advice. But they've forgotten that they struggled in their twenties too. My grandparents supported my father when he opened a business. And when it failed, my father pawned my grandmother's gold jewellery to pay off loans. Just because the last few decades were smooth on them, they think the whole world is thriving, and that it's my fault for being unemployed, which it probably is, but that shouldn't give them the license to give me a hard time. That's what is happening now too; I am a lesbian, which to my mother means I am not conventional. She will use every opportunity to punish me into becoming straight and conventional so I can be as successful as her peers. So, I can have an empty life with meaningless over-indulgence, small-talking acquaintances, and society's respect.

I'm addressing all this in the novel I am writing. I also want to explore wealth inequalities in short stories. I was packing to move out just now and got this idea: a short story where every financial transaction is done through bidding. This woman has to out-bid everyone in the city to get anything she wants.

'All the potatoes in the city,' the auctioneer says.

'Ew! Is that what a potato looks like?' A rich kid says. 'How horrid! Surely there are better looking potatoes with less dust on them!'

The friends of the son of the richest industrialist in the country who owns a house that reaches the clouds dare him to bid.

'Let me check my bank account... I only have eighty-five crore rupees, guys,' the scion says, 'Eight thousand for all the potatoes in the city.'

'Sold to the scion!'

Okay, that's a bit ridiculous. The story I'd write (or not) will be subtler. I was thinking today that every city I am in, I am attending an auction with the rich people of that city. Every bag of potato I have ever bought was thanks to a rich person who didn't outbid me for it. The story is a hyperbolic take on contemporary capitalism. It's not even hyperbolic if you think of potatoes as a metaphor for a square-foot of land in the city.

Owning a few square-feet of land would be great though. It's my life's dream to own a house and never leave it. Or rent a house and never leave it. I just want to be in a house. I've moved homes at least 15 times till now, but I never wanted to move out of any of those homes. Till I left Bombay, I moved out because my parents were moving out. With Bombay and Ahmedabad, I moved out to escape eviction.

Even after moving so many times, I am never emotionally prepared to pack all my belongings. The first time I moved was from Chennai to Bombay when I was 11. I knew about the move a year before we actually did. I was heartbroken about it, so I told all my friends that I'd be moving to Bombay in a year. I thought they'd comfort me, but they stopped investing in the friendship and started ignoring me. When my best friend came over to my house on moving day, I was ready to say goodbye. But she just wanted a book of hers that I had borrowed. I was petty: I told her I had lost it even though I had it. She frowned and left.

Moving from Chennai to Bombay threw me off completely. My parents, grandparents, brother and I moved from a 1200 sq. ft three-bedroom house in Chennai to a 600 sq. ft two-bedroom one in Bombay. It felt like my life had shrunk. I went to a shabby school, and my parents, who commuted two hours every day to work and back, were cranky all the time. My parents and grandparents fought every night, my father by the bottle insulting, my grandfather cursing, and my mother and grandmother crying for hours every night. Every night their predicament oppressed and suffocated my inner crises.

Nobody paused to explain to me that the cost of living is different in each city. I thought we'd lost a lot of money, which is why we had to move out of our roomy house in Chennai to the cramped apartment in Bombay. I thought my parents yelled at my grandparents for losing their money. I thought the reason my grandparents, brother, and I all had to sleep squeezed together in the same bed was because my grandparents got scammed or spent all the money recklessly. I began disrespecting my grandparents; after all, they were the cause of the inconvenience. Our relationship dynamic changed, and fresh out of the Chennai respect-your-elders mould, I became a rebel.

In Bombay, I felt more isolated than ever. All my classmates spoke Hindi, a language I couldn't speak or understand. I had no idea what anyone was saying. I had barely had any friends in Chennai but at least my classmates there used to speak to me.

Not so in Bombay—I spent the entire year with an intellectually disabled girl named Lalita who couldn't speak distinguishable words, and therefore couldn't speak Hindi either. She was five years older than the rest of us, but she looked much older. Since we both couldn't communicate with others in the class, we sat quietly next to each other through the school year.

My teachers thought I was good friends with Lalita and asked me a favour. They didn't explain why but they asked me to inform them if there were blood stains on her skirt. I didn't know Lalita was intellectually challenged; I thought she was dying of cancer and that's why she couldn't talk. I thought she would die if I let her bleed, so I spent the entire school year anxiously staring at her skirt. I would insist on going to school even when I was sick because I thought she would die if I wasn't there to spot the blood. My parents thought it was because I loved going to school. Eventually, I failed in every subject and was asked to repeat the school year. My parents lost their jobs, however, and found new ones in Delhi so we all moved again. I got another shot at making new friends who didn't know I was repeating my school year.

Growing up, the next move to another city was always around the corner. My father only had a job till he drunk-texted his boss/colleagues nasty things. He expected everyone to treat him like he was Steve Jobs, and it made him mad when nobody did. He was always writing nasty messages; asking us if he should hit Send just to make us say nice things to him and plead with him not to send it. But he'd hit Send often enough to lose jobs repeatedly. In 2003 we moved from Chennai to Bombay, in 2004 from Bombay to Delhi, in 2005 my father moved from Delhi to Lucknow (while we stayed in Delhi), in 2006 he moved from Lucknow to Delhi, and in 2008 we moved from Delhi to Bombay. All because of his drunk texts.

Between these moves were contemplation of moves that didn't work out. My father was an optimist, so he'd tell us he was very close to getting a job offer just after sending his resumé to a company. We thought seriously of upending our lives and moving to Singapore or Dubai or Accra or Calcutta or Delhi or Chennai or other cities every other month. Every day felt like we were just a few weeks away from moving to a new city or country—school year be damned. So, I never bothered to make friends. Why would I make a friend and then feel sad to leave them? I was smart and I thought I should save myself the misery and just not have friends. It was hard to tell when my father was being serious about a move and when he was just stroking his own ego. I remained the quiet one in the class who avoided others. I learnt to live with myself, pack my bags quickly and move cities with no notice.

When my parents weren't talking about moving out of the house, they were busy trying to destroy the house. Like the time my mother had a hundred purple pinch marks on her left shoulder or the time our house was filled with pools of blood when my father got stitches on his chin or the time my brother had swollen knuckles from punching the wall in a mad rage. We had a brawl in our house every night. Every single night. Often somebody threatened to hit someone else. Sometimes somebody actually hit another person and we were left hiding scars or rushing to the hospital for stitches. I was the peacemaker; everybody liked me because I made everybody like me because I was too scared to throw a punch.

After my family fell asleep, I'd stay up worrying how I was going to react if my father, in his drunkenness, killed my mother, or my mother or brother, in a fit of rage, killed my father. Would I help them get rid of the body? Would I go to the police? Would the police suspect me? I used to practise talking to the police, I used to try to rehearse the right words and facial expressions to make the truth sound more believable.

'I am sorry I never complained to the police about the domestic abuse happening in my house,' I rehearsed. 'My mother said her parents were heart patients and if I complained, it would break their hearts and kill them. I didn't want to kill my grandparents. I love my family.' Then I'd fake a tear. (I've gotten really good at fake-crying, fooled my parents many times) I rehearsed some more, 'I just miss my father/mother/brother so much.'

Eventually, I got to a point where I didn't care who died, I just didn't want to deal with the dead body. I spent a lot of time reading news articles about domestic homicides, looking for differences between their circumstances and my family's brawls. There was no difference. My family members were all short-tempered and at the threshold of losing control quite often. I kept practising my sad face look, hoping I'd never have to use it.

What really unnerved me was how fast everything became 'normal' the next morning. One night after a feverish fight, my brother ran away from home. My mother and I searched for him on the streets till late in the night while my father stayed home, drinking. We later found my brother crying in the parking lot. I thought he had left to kill himself. I couldn't sleep that night; I was traumatised at the thought of losing him, just like that, after a terrible night. But the next morning, my mother came to our room with the widest smile, with overblown enthusiasm, waking me up, and talking to me like nothing bad had ever happened. If I tried to tell her I was upset about the previous night, she'd get upset, ask me to get over it and stop making a big deal. So, I started mirroring her: forced wide smiles, a manic lust for life that'd wear off in a few minutes. Soon it started becoming a habit even outside home. I behaved the same way with a friend in school, started smiling and acting normal with her immediately after an argument, and she made me realise how weird it was. After that, I had to tutor myself to stay upset and reconcile. But my first instinct was still to pretend everything was perfect. I got so good at keeping secrets, living a double life, I didn't know how to stop.

I have been moving out all my life, but it feels like I've never moved out, because I haven't moved out in the way it would matter to me. Ever since I can remember, from when I was eight years old or so, I couldn't wait to grow up and move out of my parents' house and their shadow. I have been dreaming about emancipation for as long as I can remember. I was always plotting grand plans to run away from home. I did it once when I was 12, the year we lived in Bombay. Even though I never believed in religion, I ran away to live in a temple—planning to eat the temple offerings and survive. My brother, who was 8 at the time, followed me to the temple that day. He cried for an hour, pleading with me to come back. People stared at me on the street, and a couple of people asked my brother why he was crying. I thought I'd go back home and attempt to run away again later, this time without saying goodbye to my brother. But we moved cities a month after, and I never found a temple so generous with its offerings after that.

At 14, I was obsessed with running away from the house again. So obsessed that it was all I thought about. It would have helped me if I had thought of careers or jobs, but I didn't care what I was doing as long as I was living on my own. After I finished school, I enrolled to become a Chartered Accountant. The course had a three-year articleship period with a compulsory stipend that gave me a chance to get away from the house.

But after I started the articleship, I noticed that I exhibited a few symptoms of dyslexia. I went through a test at 20 that confirmed it. I realised that I couldn't finish the Chartered Accountancy course in the first attempt because my brand of dyslexia made it hard for me to memorise tax laws. I couldn't fail while living in my parents' house so I gave up Accountancy along with my plans to run away, and thought seriously about a career that was possible without dyslexia ruining it for me. I spent two years learning computer programming and working for a cinema house, but after coming out at 22, I was fleeing again.

I have been dreaming of a home forever. I always knew a nurturing and stable house was all I needed to thrive. But I didn't know how to get there. When I was 12, I tried putting myself up for adoption, even thought of writing to Angelina Jolie and Madonna to adopt me. But I wasn't a baby, or a cute adolescent. I kept harbouring this dream of a stable and nurturing home till it became an obsession.

I keep thinking that when I have my own home, I'll never leave the place. But I don't think I will ever have a home. A home is too steady a structure to sustain in a city. I would go broke and lose my job a dozen times before I could afford even a tiny little flat. And knowing Indian cities, even before I move into the flat, there'd be a new flyover passing by it, a railway station in front of it and eight high-rise buildings around it where my parents would buy their sixth home. I cannot imagine writing novels with the constant noise of drilling and hammering around me. I guess I can never have a home the way I imagine it.

My home can only exist as a fixed structure in my mind, fixed in architecture and space, and even in its inhabitants because so far it only hosts me. My lofty little home exists in me. No land holds us, so we keep moving in cars and trains, and we rest on a borrowed chair or a cheap, used mattress—any makeshift land I can afford for my lofty little dream. With means or not, I don't think I trust the land beneath me to hold me anymore. Every time something doesn't go my way, my first instinct is to move out: hit refresh and start over in a new city. No matter how comfortable I get, before I know it, I'd be on moving wheels again, reluctant, but also happy to get away. Like I'll be tomorrow when I board the train. Like I'll be always.

3. Moving

I am moving. I couldn't afford to send all my belongings through a Mover so I donated my books, clothes, and other stuff that I didn't want to carry. I sent my scooter through a Mover and I have two suitcases that I'm lugging around, one in each hand. I also suffer from dysgraphia, a writing disorder that sometimes accompanies dyslexia, which affects fine motor skills. It makes me drop things, gives me a weird grip, and tires my fingers very fast. It was difficult for me to climb up and down the stairs at the station carrying two suitcases. My fingers gave up and I dropped the suitcases many times, even watched them go thumping down the steps. People gave me a dirty look like I was a capable person being clumsy, like I was intoxicated or something.

I bet they wouldn't look at me that way if I had hand braces on. Anyway, I don't care—not about the people, not about the suitcase. There was nothing in it worth caring for, just old faded clothes.

I'm sitting on a suitcase now, waiting for the train. I try not to think that nobody said goodbye, nobody came to the station to help me, and nobody is going to call me and ask if I feel okay. My mother might, I guess. She'll call me tomorrow and pretend like she tried to reach my phone the day before and the call didn't go through. That's what happens when your caring comes from a sense of duty, from a compulsion to be seen as a good mother, and not from your heart. I've lived so long, I should matter to somebody, no? Sitting here, alone, two hours early for my train, with two suitcases: I feel vulnerable. What if something happens to me? Nobody is with me, nobody is talking to me—Who's going to come looking for me?

I wanted to travel by the ordinary non-AC sleeper class compartment, but my mother offered to pay for the AC sleeper ticket. I said yes, although I should have said no. I was tempted for one last whiff of comfort before I was swarmed by mosquitoes again. Now that my mother has paid for an AC ticket, she will use it against me and get me to do something she wants. I think she wants me to attend my grandparents' 60th anniversary celebrations as part of the family. I know she has been bribing my brother for it.

I would have travelled by sleeper class if it wasn't so sad. Comfort-wise, the AC class just has the AC over the sleeper class, and I don't mind sleeping in a pool of my own sweat. I'm just uncomfortable with all those people who board the sleeper class without tickets and sit on the train floor. They sit on filth and sleep on the floor with dirty shoes as pillows. If there were no suitcase under the seat, they roll under the seat that probably hasn't been cleaned since 1980, that has dirt mixed with oil mixed with every strain of bacteria imaginable, and they sleep there all night. I was horrified looking at people sleeping that way when I travelled by sleeper class at 11, in 2004. I remember accidently stepping on so many people on my way to the bathroom (which was filthy) and they didn't so much as wince. I wondered then why they needed to travel at all, if they had to travel that way. Only when I saw Bombay slums that were located a hair's breadth away from running sewage water did I realise that their homes might not be drastically different from that train floor.

I pity myself now, sitting in the AC compartment, by the window, watching the landscape shift like it was happening to someone else. It feels like I'm watching a screen showing a video of changing landscapes. It is sad that I am experiencing movement this way. I would have liked to climb up and sit on the train's roof, with the violent air hitting my face. I'd watch people watch me as I pass by soaking in the moment, odours, and sounds. I would internalise the velocity as the train moved faster and faster till I felt sick and dizzy. That would have been the right way to experience the movement, right here and now. But instead, I am stuck in a kind of torpor, my emotional response to the situation delayed and cushioned by air-conditioned comforts. I shall feel the velocity of movement soon, in the new city, in a tiny room, alone, in the middle of the night. And then I'll wonder what caused it.

I think half of my problems stem from not internalising movement. I moved from city to city without ever thinking why I was moving. I just took a flight and in an hour I lived in another city, all the time just thinking about the inconvenience of those tiny flight seats. Why did I leave Bombay? I don't know. Was I fleeing from the memory of the confrontation I had had with my mother? Had I outgrown Bombay's largeness? Did I not believe it was the city of dreams anymore? After I came out, my mother moved out without paying the electricity bill, and I didn't want to talk to her about it so I borrowed money from a friend to pay it. Was that why I left? I knew that paying the rent and electricity bill would bankrupt me. I knew I had no future in Bombay that didn't involve me struggling to make ends meet.

Or did I leave because I realised the freedom that I felt in Bombay was just other people's indifference to me and not really freedom? I was not free because others were championing my freedom; I was not free because of an inclusive mindset. I was free because nobody fucking cared. My neighbours didn't know my name. My domestic help never spoke to me, she left the moment she was done cleaning. Nobody cared if I lived or died. I've done that myself, casually driven past several pedestrian or bike accidents on my way to work, ignoring people who needed help. Broken limbs on the road was just a speed breaker for me. I was only worried about missing the traffic signal and being late to work. I couldn't even see a doctor about my sinus attacks—there was no time. I had to work, pay rent, rinse, and repeat.

Maybe I left because of both reasons—realising I can never afford Bombay and realising the 'city of dreams' spiel was a sham. I can only guess this now, a year later. That's why I travel by train these days. (not that I could afford flights). Travelling by train takes enough time waiting and doing nothing to reach the destination. Enough to force me to have thoughts about where I was going and what I was leaving behind. Sometimes that can be a bad thing, like right now, when I'm forced to think that I am leaving behind nothing and going to nothing. I chose to do a Master's degree to live in a public hostel rent-free. After abandoning accountancy, I thought I might as well get a degree in writing. At least I know I like writing. I chose Communications for my Master's instead of English because the Communications department was usually clubbed with the fine arts department, unlike English which was clubbed with language or social science departments. I chose Communications over English to be closer to the fine arts department because I'd rather date an artist than a scholar. I'm doing the degree to live rent-free and find love. That's the grand design behind my career choices.

I've gone soft since I met Bhavya. I had a girlfriend once, and that makes me think I might have one again. Although there was a time, I was happy alone—when I was 16 and wasn't sexually interested in anyone; it felt oddly empowering. I used to tell myself that I didn't like anyone because nobody was good enough for me. I used to ooze self-importance and arrogance. I was big back then, and the world was small. I was bigger than my family, my school, my college. Now, it's different. I have been drowning in the job market for three years and I feel small and replaceable, and the world looks so big that I hate it. In my youth, I would disobey, travel without a ticket, I would stand tall around people whose lives (I would think) radically changed because they were in a train with me and my largeness. I would take pride in looking strong, cold and unapproachable. Now I am in an air-conditioned compartment looking timid. I wouldn't dare travel without a ticket or in an environment unsafe for me. I wouldn't dare travel at all if the ground beneath me didn't move.

My thoughts about my hardcore youth days are

interrupted by the Gujarati family across from me, already wanting to sleep at 7 pm. They want me to lie down too so they can pitch the middle berth. I tell them I won't lie down till 9, at least. Now ladies in the family are lying down opposite me and two men sit next to me, waiting with me for the clock to strike 9. They are exhausted from playing card games and singing Bollywood songs. They had dinner at 6: an entire bag full of food that they distributed to each other; they dropped some on the floor to feed the mice too. They were so pleased with me when I told them I had studied accounting that I didn't tell them I had quit. The old man said his son was also studying accounting, pointing to a young lad with a thin adolescent moustache smiling at me. The young lad tried to make conversation with me about the stock market. I told him that I had invested heavily in Reliance companies. He was pleased. He waited for me to ask him about his stock preferences. I didn't and let the conversation die.

I marvelled at the way the family settled into the train booth like it was their own home. They used their suitcase as a table to play cards. They used the lower berth on the side as space for placing the food and plates. They hung cotton sheets where the women slept to give them privacy and used an extension cord to charge all their phones from the single railway plug point. How could they warm up to this space and get so comfortable here?

I always feel like an impostor, no matter where I am. I am so conscious not to change my surroundings even when I am living somewhere, as though I have no business being there, as though I would adulterate it by doing so. I feel like a guest in someone's house all the time, being watchful not to disrupt their home. I think it comes from living in rented houses all my life; even when I lived in the house owned by my parents, to me, it felt much like a rented house.

Maybe I always felt like an outsider physically from being continuously made to feel like an outsider mentally. I always felt alienated from those around me because I wasn't like them and I didn't know why. I was the only one in my friend circle who mixed up the alphabets d, g, p, and b in her late teens. I was the only one who wasn't attracted to boys. I didn't know anyone who was like me, not in real life, not anecdotally, and not in the fiction or movies I was exposed to. So I spent 20 years not knowing that it was okay to be a lesbian and that it was okay to be dyslexic: that it wasn't my fault for not trying hard enough, it was just the way my brain and body were wired. Instead, I hid my true self, pretended everything was fine, lying about it all because I couldn't explain who I was. I have never let my guard down, never let me be myself completely. I'd spend my time like I am spending my time on this train. Taking as little space as possible, lying about who I am, and waiting for it to get over. I think I'll spare these gentlemen some misery and go to bed.

*

It's morning now. I didn't sleep at all. Got a terrible headache. The Gujarati family tried to make conversation with me again; I'm pretending to write so they leave me alone. Sorry to them for being rude, but I'm not comfortable being myself in front of these people so I don't want to waste my time pretending to be someone else for them. Now they peer into my notebook every time they get up so I have to keep writing or they'll call my bluff and I shall be forced to talk to them. If I am forced to scribble, I might as well write about the novel I'm planning.

The novel is about Namrata, a 24-year-old

woman, who wants to leave her middle-class comforts to live in a poor neighbourhood and write philosophy. Namrata is disgusted by her money-hungry, status-conscious family and believes that materialistic pleasures are impurities that corrupt the mind. She wants to do physical labour and live with limited means to understand humanity better for her philosophy.

Through this story, I want to explore the different aspects of living in a poor neighbourhood to see for myself if it might suit me. I've been obsessed about living in poor neighbourhoods since I started fantasising about running away from home. To me, the greatest thing I can achieve is to survive while paying as little rent as possible. If I can manage my whole life in fifteen thousand rupees a month, I can confidently tell my parents what I think of them and get them out of my life completely. No more formalities, no more smiling for family portraits. I am confident I can make fifteen thousand rupees a month one way or the other, even if I keep losing jobs. It's the only way I'd never need my parents to lend me any money. It's the only way to be completely independent, and I'm obsessed with the idea.

I also want to explore how realistic it is for someone to actually climb down the socio-economic ladder. I think once a person is used to certain privileges and comforts, it would be incredibly difficult to live without them. Such a person will use whatever favours and connections they have at their disposal to retain the comforts. Peers from my socio-economic background would never live in the hostel of an Indian public university, and that is exactly what I am about to do. I know living in a poor neighbourhood is different from living in a public university hostel, but I think the latter is a tiny dose of the former. Public university hostels are known to be dingy. In the university I am attending, I'd have to share a shower and toilet with 10 other students. That's the biggest challenge for me: sharing space with strangers with whom I don't share the same politics, interests, and values. I want to see how I can cope.

But the novel I'm writing is not about me; it's about Namrata whose upbringing was more comfortable than mine and who was not forced out of the house but chose to leave it. I feel the toughest part of it would be to accurately relate the details of the protagonist's motives. That's the entire story—it's got to be convincing. The capitalist angst angle works to some extent. But is it strong enough to choose a noisy, cramped, sketchy dwelling over a comfortable house in a well-kept neighbourhood?

Maybe I would know the motive once I am in the story—living in the hostel. I could always make my protagonist a lesbian, but no publisher would risk signing this novel (would they otherwise?), with it being 2016 and gay sex being illegal and all. I wouldn't be writing at all if I cared what publishers think. But I don't want Namrata to be a lesbian and get disowned by her family—forced to choose a life of fewer means out of compulsion. I want to write about a character who chooses her own destiny; that's more interesting and I'd actually want to write about it. It would make me forget about my situation and maybe I too will believe I chose the destiny of sharing a toilet with 10 strangers for some convoluted reason that I would finally figure out when I am on the commode.

4. Enrolling

I took a cab from the railway station to the university. The admission process took several hours of waiting in lines. While I waited, I realised that a lot of students already knew each other. I talked to a group who told me they knew each other from studying in the same Bachelor's college. A few waited by themselves like I did. Once I was done with the admission formalities, I headed to the hostel building that was assigned to me and showed my admission slip to the warden. I asked her if I could get a single room.

'Not possible. We only give single rooms to PhD scholars.'

'I need it because I have dyslexia. I can't study

when there is a lot of noise around me. I got admission through the disability quota—'

'Oh like *Taare Zameen Par*?' She said, her face lit up.

'Um, yeah, I have issues… like that boy.'

She asked me to wait. She probably thought I'd wait for 20 minutes and leave, and she could stall for another day. I sat in her room and started reading a book like I had nowhere else to be. Now, I am writing.

Fucking *Taare Zameen Par*. Every person asks me if I am like that boy in the film when I tell them I am dyslexic. It's as it is hard to explain what dyslexia is and that film made it harder. The boy in the film probably had a combination of attention-deficit hyperactive disorder (ADHD), dyspraxia, dyscalculia, and dyslexia and the film swept it all under dyslexia without giving each condition any individual attention. The scriptwriter/director was probably too busy adding melodrama.

My mother cried buckets watching that film, she felt so bad for the poor dyslexic boy. A few years later when I told her I showed symptoms of dyslexia, she was in denial and as unsympathetic as the boy's father in the film. She said I can't have dyslexia because I'm not dumb. Anyway, it doesn't matter what she said. It matters that I studied in four schools, at least 50 teachers taught me and nobody noticed I wrote *g* instead of *d*. I used to love English class, especially when it involved writing essays. I always expected the teachers to give me feedback on my flair for writing and ideas, but I only got feedback on my spelling mistakes. I stopped showing anyone what I wrote.

When I first watched *Taare Zameen Par*, I didn't know I was dyslexic and the film didn't help me realise it one bit. I realised I was dyslexic while studying for the Chartered Accountancy Intermediate course, also called CA Inter, which was the second-level of the three-level Chartered Accountant course. I thought I could be a good accountant because I had a knack for bookkeeping which came as easily as logical thinking to me. But being an accountant also meant knowing tax laws—and I just couldn't rote learn them. I couldn't remember if the house rent allowance was exempt under section 10(13a) or 13(10a) or 130(a) just like I can't remember if 'fridge' is spelled frigde or fridge. I remember the house rent allowance rule is the minimum of actual allowance or x% of salary or excess of rent paid over x% of salary. I just can't remember the 'x' numbers in the rule because it is an arbitrary number that the government chose as appropriate for calculating taxes—nothing logical or sensible about it. And there were almost a hundred such rules like house rent allowance, all with their arbitrary numbers that I couldn't remember.

I spent much of 2010 and 2011 at home studying for the accountancy exams. My father was unemployed for much of that time and he'd feel so worthless sitting at home on his own that he'd get drunk every night and rave about how I'd fail my papers and come crawling to him to help me make a career just to boost his own ego. My ego told me I should rather die than fail those papers and face my father in disgrace. I used to get panic attacks at 2 am thinking I'll fail the tax paper, and I used to run on the treadmill we had at home for half an hour in the middle of the night just to tire out my flight or fight response.

I cleared the exams in the first attempt, and scored exact passing marks in the tax paper. But I knew there was no way I could pass the final paper that had even more tax laws to rote learn. All the while I knew others in my accountancy class thought tax was easy. Frustrated, I searched online if others found tax laws difficult too. I found a quote by Albert Einstein: The hardest thing in the world to understand is the income tax. I don't know what he meant by that, but I remembered that Einstein was thought to be dyslexic. So I searched for dyslexia symptoms and suspected I could be dyslexic too. I approached a hospital to get tested, but they needed my parent's signature to test me even though I was 20 years old. I told my parents and they thought it was an excuse to quit accountancy. Thankfully the test was cheap so they agreed to let me take it just to shut me up.

I was nervous before my dyslexia assessment tests. I read that dyslexic people don't do well in standardised tests, just like me, and I didn't know if taking a standardised test to assess dyslexia was an effective strategy. After a psychiatric evaluation, the assessment involved an IQ test and a language skills test. But already after the psychiatric evaluation, the psychiatrist told me that I probably don't have dyslexia because I didn't exhibit the classic dyslexia symptoms like confusing left from right, wearing the left shoe on the right feet, etc., the way my brother did. He diagnosed me with general anxiety and clinical depression, and he was more concerned about those issues. But he prescribed the remaining tests for me anyway just to be sure.

The remaining tests included one to measure my intelligence and compare it to the average human intelligence and one that compared my language skill levels with the average skill levels of each age group. A person with dyslexia would score much better in the IQ test than the language skills test which would mean that their language skills, like reading and writing, don't reflect their actual intelligence.

I took the Wechsler Adult Intelligence Scale IQ test. My verbal IQ that measured my ability to analyse information and solve problems was 131. My psychiatrist said that it meant I had a gifted intellectual capacity that only the top 2% of the population shared. My performance IQ that measured my ability to process and interpret symbols was 114, still well above the average IQ of 100 points. It was clear that parts of my brain weren't doing as well as the rest. It was also clear that I wasn't as stupid as I felt when I spelt the word 'and' as 'ang'.

The language skills test had many reading and writing exercises. To judge my writing skills, I was asked to write about my happiest memory. At that time, sitting at the testing centre, all I could think of were memories with Bhavya: our long walks in South Bombay; the way she held me while we rode on my scooter; the way we used to run recklessly down the stairs, across the local platform, to catch a moving train together. But I didn't want to write about Bhavya and confuse the person who was assessing my skills. They'd probably think I was so bad at writing that I was writing about a boy but it read like I was writing about a girl, that I even spelled the name wrong. So I wrote about a memory when I was driving alone from Andheri to Kandivali to see Bhavya. I had been writing fiction that day and feeling ecstatic. And I was driving to see her in the evening when it was already dark and as I went up and down the flyovers in the Eastern Express Highway, the tiny red dots of car brake lights were shining like the stars in the sky. It was beautiful, but yeah, not a very happy-happy memory.

When I wrote about it at the test, I was asked to write by hand. I had to work with my very limited writing vocabulary of four-letter, and the occasional five-letter, words that I could spell. My first sentence was about the lights and after I wrote it, I realised that I forgot to mention that it was evening or even where I was. I wrote about that in the second sentence. My third sentence was about how happy I felt, but I hadn't talked about writing fiction yet to explain the happiness. I should have started my essay with the bit about writing fiction and then talked about the day and then talked about the moment—but it was all inked out and too late. I can't order or structure sentences properly because of the writing disorder I suffer from, dysgraphia.

Just taking the test made me feel defeated and helpless. It felt like I was talking with a sock in my mouth; the few words I inked out were incoherent and nonsensical. If I could have written on a laptop, I would have done a better job moving the sentences around and using spell-check to write more appropriate and telling words. But I was forced to write by hand, like I wrote all my exams, and each experience writing by hand was traumatic. By writing by hand that day, I witnessed myself butcher a happy memory.

At the age of 20 when I took the language skills test, most of my language skills were at the average levels of 16- or 17-year-olds. My writing skills were comparable with the skill level of a 14-year-old. A 14-year-old! I was crushed! I abandoned my plans to write a novel and instead did online courses on designing and building websites. Then I took the cinema house job. But I couldn't resist the thought of writing, and kept writing anyway. But every day that I wrote, I kept thinking my writing was sub-par.

The doctors should have told me in detail what the tests meant, but instead they just told me that I had dyslexia and dysgraphia. When I asked the psychiatrist why he had earlier thought I wasn't dyslexic, he said because he hadn't expected me to be intellectually gifted. It didn't strike me as odd at that time but when I think about it now, I think he meant that my language skills were somewhat average and so he thought I wasn't dyslexic because only those with poor language skills usually have dyslexia, which I think implies that only those with average or poor IQ have dyslexia. Funny, the doctor would share the misconception that dyslexics can't be intelligent, just like when I tell people I have dyslexia and they say—but, you are so intelligent—like they are mutually exclusive things.

When I asked him how to cope with dyslexia, he said I was too old to learn how to cope. When I asked him what dyslexia was, he said: it is when someone has trouble reading and spelling. When I pointed out that having trouble reading and spelling were symptoms of dyslexia and not dyslexia itself, he said dyslexia is a reading disorder, which is the noun form of 'having trouble reading', still just a symptom.

I don't have a degree in psychiatry but from what I've noticed in myself and my brother who is also dyslexic, I think dyslexia is the disorder of abstraction. When I see the word dog, there is a very specific arrangement of letters that makes the very specific word. If I abstract the word and remove the specificity of the position and orientation of letters, I get god, bob, dob, bod, and so on from the word dog. When I think of the word dog, I have an abstract image of the different shapes of letters that make the word. That's my first language—an abstract notion. Every time I have to write the word dog, I have to translate that abstract notion into a specific position and orientation of the shapes of the English alphabet. I'm unable to make that translation quickly and correctly—that's the disorder. It takes time and I have a tendency to get it wrong.

It's the same with directions. I am actually pretty good at navigating; I can easily get from one point to another. Every time I go to Sarojini Nagar Market with my family, I can easily navigate back to where we parked our car. But if I'm asked to help someone else navigate by giving them directions, it is difficult for me to translate the abstract notion into words. I'm terrible at giving and understanding directions.

Imagine the mind of a person who translates every object, subject, emotion, and encounter into an abstract notion. The kind of connections the mind can make when you remove the mundane specificity, when you strip down the unnecessary details, are limitless. But I'm pushed to focus more and more on the translation to detailed and specific terms so that others can understand. I find the more time I spend in the abstract world, on my own, in my head, the harder it gets to translate. I often feel isolated and in a state where I don't want to communicate or even process information.

When I read, I can't detect and process individual alphabets (symbols) into words very elegantly. What I do instead: I look at the word and recall words in my vocabulary that look the most like that word. My brain doesn't do a text search for the word, it does a text-based image search. This makes it incredibly difficult for me to correctly read: words that look very similar to other words (especially if they have multiple Gs, Ds, Ps, and Bs) and unfamiliar words that are not in my vocabulary (most proper nouns). And reading like this is so difficult and exhausting, I skim a lot. Take this book I have with me that I was planning on reading while I was waiting for the warden to assign me a room. I have been recommended this book so many times that I was curious to read it. It's called *The God of Small Things* and it is authored by Arundathi Roy. Here are the starting lines:

'May in Ayemenem is a hot, brooding month. The days are long and humid. The river shrinks and black crows gorge on bright mangoes in still, dustgreen trees. Red bananas ripen. Jackfruits burst. Dissolute bluebottles hum vacuously in the fruity air.'

This is how I read it:

'May in A_____ is a hot, brooding month. The river shrinks and black crows dodge mangoes in trees. Desolate bluebottoms hum vicariously in the fruity air.'

I'm missing so many pieces of the puzzle, I'm imagining dodgy crows and blue-bottomed baboons. I generally hate writing that tries to paint a picture with words like we are living in the 16th century without high-resolution pictures and film. If I wanted to perceive the visual beauty of fruits and trees, I'd watch a documentary or an arthouse film in 4K resolution, not read a book when reading one is so difficult for me. I prefer books that describe the beating heart, but such books are rare.

This book also has too many unfamiliar words that are not in my vocabulary like so many books by Indian writers. They write in fancy English like we all lived in England in the Victorian era. It is almost like a British person visited India and wrote the book. I steer away from British and Indian writers and I find it easier to read English translations of Russian, German, and French authors. I've never read Shakespeare. I'm sure he is great, but his writing is not accessible to my mind.

Even the books I do read, I barely finish them. If I can't read the book in a week, there is no point getting back to it as I've already forgotten the characters, their names, and how they are related to each other. It's pointless, I might as well start again. Reading feels like a punishment to me even now. I get a headache just from reading a few pages, with all that image-based word search and translation going on in my head. I hold a book in my hands and ask myself why I am putting myself through the torture. But I love books, and I engage very well with written narratives. But imagine my sense of self-worth as a writer who thinks reading is a punishment. I understand the irony of being a writer with a writing disorder. But I can't help it. I have thoughts swimming around in my head that keep editing themselves into neat sentences and only leave my head when I write them down. I despair the least on days when I'm writing and I'm grateful I at least enjoy applying myself to this one thing even if it is the wrong choice for me. Maybe it's just a hobby. An all-consuming hobby.

This university reminds me of all the other educational institutions I have failed out of. I couldn't manage doing a Bachelor's in Commerce along with the Chartered Accountancy course so I dropped out of the degree after I failed two papers in the first year. I enrolled in a distance degree programme and completed my Bachelor's in Commerce. I abandoned Chartered Accountancy mid-way. I attended a semester of Master's in Economics in 2014 and failed out after the first semester.

The first semester with Economics was a disaster, as a matter of fact. I never imagined I'd have trouble with the type of things I had trouble with over there. I failed two out of four papers. Macroeconomics was the first paper I failed, mostly because the questions were worded in a way that was confusing to me. Almost every other question started as 'Which among the following statements are False:' with four complex statements which took so much effort to work out that by the time I was done, I forgot if I was looking for False statements or True statements and I'd mark False statements as True or the other way around. I still don't know if this was general dyslexia or my brand of dyslexia or dysgraphia, but just remembering if I was supposed to check a statement to be False or True while working out the statement was too much juggling for the way my brain was wired. I didn't know that till after I failed the exam.

I failed the Microeconomics paper after repeatedly mixing up the formulas and confusing the X-axis with the Y-axis and getting all my graphs wrong. The dependent variable was always on the X-axis—or was it Y-axis? I wasn't sure if I should ask the dean if I could take a retest. When I was thinking of a way I could explain my specific troubles with the exam format to her, I couldn't help but feel like I was just making excuses for my poor performance. But I thought I should try, at least; maybe she would be empathetic to my troubles.

'Wish you had told me all this before the exams,' she said. 'How can we believe you now?'

'But I didn't know I had dyslexia until a year ago,' I reasoned, 'I'm still learning about the extent and ways dyslexia affects me.'

'I'm sorry about that,' she said. 'But I can't do anything about it.'

That day I realised that I was supposed to stay ahead of dyslexia and collect proof of disability and make declarations in advance if I wanted to be believed. I had to think like a lawyer. The dean told me that I had to skip the academic year and rejoin the first semester if I wanted to continue the course. I guess she reasoned that for a dyslexic like me, it was probably okay to take five years to complete the course. She is probably right, but my parents weren't going to be that patient. They are definitely too Brahmin to associate themselves with a daughter who took five years to complete a two-year Master's programme. Even if I rejoined the course, I'd probably have the same issues again. The dean made no promises to change the question format or make it possible for me to take an oral test.

My experience with the attempt at doing a Master's in Economics made me swear off the traditional education route again. Which is why I can't take myself seriously at this university. I keep telling myself that I'm here to live rent-free because I can't tell myself that I'm here for a degree. If I start dreaming about graduating, I'll spend every minute stressing about exams—just to get crushed again when I don't make it to the third semester. I don't even realistically think I can live rent-free here for two years because that would mean I'm passing most of the papers. I'm telling myself that doing this course in this university is a way for me to live a few months without paying rent till I figure something else out.

It sounds crazy for a person like me who has trouble reading and writing to try to get a degree in Communications. That's also why I didn't choose to study English which would have involved so much more reading and writing—and reading Shakespeare! I have avoided pursuing anything serious in reading and writing especially after the language skills test that revealed that I write like a 14-year-old. But my mind is weird in that I derive some perverse pleasure in writing—I can't help myself. After several attempts at trying to get a degree and a job in what I thought was 'logical' for me and failing, I thought why not give writing a try. I didn't expect to actually get admission in a university, although much of the credit goes to the disability quota than my abilities. Then I was homeless, so I'm here—but I don't know why and what the fuck I'm doing. I always had a strong logical reason for all my choices—this is the first time I don't, so I'm telling myself I'm here to escape rent and find love.

I've been waiting at the warden's office for four hours now. Just watched her have lunch. She asked me if I was going to the mess hall to eat. I said no. She would work faster if she knew I was starving. After lunch, she finally felt sorry for me and called the chief warden and got my single-room request sanctioned. She is now out looking for the room key. Glad I didn't have to do more convincing for the room.

I wasn't lying when I said I needed a single room because of dyslexia. Noise really makes it harder for me to focus. But I also just can't imagine sharing a room with a stranger. Growing up, I shared a room with my brother till I was 22 years old. All that time was spent in great distress, sharing a room with him and his untreated ADHD, and his untreated anxiety that was worsened by the undiagnosed ADHD, dyslexia, and dysgraphia. And all the while suffering from my own brand of anxiety worsened by undiagnosed dyslexia and dysgraphia. Exams made me anxious enough, and studying for them involved copious amounts of reading which was hard too—it all happened while my brother dribbled a ball around our room throughout the day in a feverish frenzy while he fast-talked non-stop about his 'plan of the month' towards his bright future as a tennis player or a scientist or a wrestler or a mathematician or a researcher. He just couldn't sit still and silent for a few seconds. Even when he'd do his homework, he'd talk to himself out loud or make nonsensical noises.

It became impossible to hear my own thoughts when my brother was around. He used to sleep by 10, so I'd start studying at 10:01 and stay up till 2 or 4 or as late as 6 when he'd wake up. When I had school, I'd wake up at 8 and catch a nap in the classroom or the bus or train. When I started college and didn't have class till noon, I'd sleep through the day till 11 or 12, waking up intermittently and tossing in bed uncomfortably through the sounds of my family's brisk, unbridled morning enthusiasm and my mother's cheap speakers that blaringly played M.S.Subbulakshmi's *Vishnu Sahasranamam* or *Suprabhatham* on repeat. When I'd finally wake up, I was told repeatedly that I'd fail in life for being the bird that overslept and didn't catch the worm. My sleep cycle was so completely off after 22 years of my bizarre sleep patterns, I still can't go to sleep before 2 in the morning.

What if I get a roommate with unhinged anxiety too? We'll keep amping up each other's anxiety till our minds pace around in anxious loops like headless chickens. My parents would do that, and it got so bad that once my mother kept hitting herself on her forehead and wouldn't stop so we had to pour a bucket of water on her head. I can't deal with that again. I'm still not a functional human being, I need peace and quiet to become one.

And would it be better if my roommate didn't suffer from anxiety? When I imagine it, it reminds me of my father who was on medication to treat his obsessive compulsive disorder, but one day he was so unsettled by the calm in his head that he panicked that the calm was changing him and threw his medicine in the dustbin. Will I also lose my shit to the calm? Any type of person is terrible for me. And it's better to be in the habit of living alone and being comfortable on my own. I think I'm going to be doing that for a long time.

5. Moving In

I was assigned Room 216 on the first floor of Ladies Hostel 1. My wing consisted of five rooms—215 through 220, a sink, a wash basin, a toilet, and a bathroom. The wing opened into a narrow corridor with Room 218 straight ahead, Rooms 219 and 220 on the right and 215 on the left, the corridor leading to the wash area, a sink area, and another brief passage on the left in the end, which led to my Room 216 with Room 217 on the right. Literally within two feet outside my door were the doors of Rooms 217 and 218.

I had to walk past 215 and the wash area to get to my room. I passed by a century-old, three-foot-long geyser above the sink, thinking that its combustion was surely going to be a subject of my nightmares.

When I first got to my room, its door was ajar, and the floor, table, and bed were covered in dust. I stood by the door, holding my suitcase for a few minutes, considering if I should first clean the room before I take my suitcase inside.

The room was L-shaped, not more than 35 square feet in all, closer to the size of a bathroom than a regular room. It was a single room because there was only one wall that was long enough for a bed, not because of the warden's benevolence towards students with learning disabilities. The walls were covered in a brown-black layer of what seemed like mould. The bed was just a thin steel sheet with legs. I spread a newspaper over the bed. When I put my suitcase on it, it made a loud squeaking noise like the sound of plastic bottles being crushed. The closet space was four by four feet, two feet deep; it reminded me of the cabinet in my parents' Bombay house above the washing machine where we kept the clothing detergent. A thin sheet with a wood laminate, metal legs and three drawers and a cane-woven steel-framed chair resembled desks and chairs I'd seen in Indian movies from the 1980s. Everything squeaked when touched, not unlike me.

How long before I get an allergy attack? I am

allergic to dust, mould, and pigeon feathers. I get breathless easily from them—once my blood oxygen levels dropped under 60 mmHg, and I had to be hospitalised. Right now, just looking at the room is making me breathless. I should probably tie a cloth around my face while I clean it. I tried to lock the door and realised that the door didn't close all the way; it was too big for the frame. Carrying my laptop bag out with me I went to see the warden about the door.

'Yeah, the doors sometimes swell up from humidity. It'll close once it stops raining,' the warden said.

'That could take months. How am I supposed to stay in the room without closing the door?'

'It's a girls' hostel. Nothing will happen,' she said.

'I have a Macbook, what if it gets stolen?'

'Put it in the cupboard and lock the cupboard when you leave for class.'

'I don't own a lock,' I said. Why didn't I bring a lock?

'Get it from the store,' she said, looking annoyed.

'The store is three kilometers away. Can't carry my laptop bag for three kilometers and back, on foot, in the rain.'

She sighed, opened her cupboard, and gave me a lock. She said, 'Return this when you buy a lock.'

As I walked back into the hostel building, I saw one of my classmates with her mother, walking out.

'Were you also assigned to this godawful building?' She asked.

'Yeah and my door doesn't shut! How is your room?'

'There is no way I'm staying in this place,' she said. 'It is so depressing. There are wires poking out of the walls. The trees are growing into the rooms. It's so dark and dingy. Makes my skin crawl.'

'Where are you going to stay?'

'The warden told us that the other hostels are much better, especially the ones on the south side. I'm going to see those. If it doesn't work out, I am just going to live outside campus and commute to class.'

'Good luck! Let me know how you find the other hostels,' I said.

Back in the room, I noticed that the switchboard was on the verge of falling out. When I peeped inside the hole between the switchboard and the wall, I could see decades of dust and a trail of ants. The fan regulator was broken and I could see open wires inside it. A few switches were new, a few were old and burnt. The wiring of the hostel was at least 30 years old. I was worried I'd electrocute myself from touching the switches. I wondered if the switchboard would blow up if I used an extension cord and charged my phone and laptop at the same time. Probably.

Staying in the room made me feel restless so I locked my valuables and stepped out. Maybe I could get coffee somewhere? I saw a girl from 218 leaving as well.

'Do you have internet on your phone?' she asked in broken Hindi.

'Yes.'

'Can you check the university website and tell me if I got a seat?' she asked. 'MBA hospital management, check the scheduled caste section.'

'What's your name?'

'Oh sorry, it's Saisree.'

'Yeah, your name is first on the scheduled caste list,' I said. 'Congratulations!'

'Thank you!' She smiled.

'How did you get this room without knowing your result?'

'This room is my friend's who is doing her MPhil

in Telugu,' she said. 'I have been living here for six months.'

'Oh, so you can stay here even if you are not enrolled?'

'It's not allowed, but girls from our village stay here sometimes,' she said. 'This is an old hostel; the warden doesn't care if you break the rules here. You can invite girls from your village or your friends to stay in your room. You can even bring an induction cooktop and cook food in your room.'

'So how many of you stay here?' I asked her.

'Six of us.'

I asked her where I could get coffee, even though with dyslexia I can't understand directions; I just wanted to end the conversation. I stopped by the toilet before leaving. It was an Indian-style commode; I had never used one, and I wasn't sure which direction to squat in. The toilet was so narrow that when I squatted, my knees touched the dirty wall tiles, making me squirm. The commode was covered in faeces-coloured stains, and it had a terrible smell, much of which was coming from the open garbage bin outside. It smelled like the menses of a hundred women combined with the smell of stale food, and the smell of general garbage. I was pretty sure having an open garbage bin in a public bathroom was a health hazard; I should complain, I thought. I buried my nose inside my t-shirt, my stench had never felt so sweet.

The whole toilet ordeal made me more restless. I was prepared to share the bathroom with 10 others, but based on what Saisree had said, I guessed there might be more girls on my floor. Maybe I should change hostels. Maybe the rooms in other hostels had doors that closed, a decent-looking geyser, a more sanitary washroom situation. Or at least one of the three. Or at least the room would be bigger, or the hostel might be less crowded. I went to speak to the warden again.

'Can I have a room in a different hostel, please?'

'Why, what's wrong with this hostel?'

I didn't want to rat out Saisree's friends so I stammered something about the wires and the smell.

'The other hostel rooms are really big, so you won't get a single room there,' she said. 'Is that okay? How will you cope with your *Taare Zameen Par* problem?

'Are you sure I can't get a single room in other hostels?'

'Not possible,' she said. 'As it is, we have more students than rooms to put them in.'

'Never mind, then,' I said.

I complained about the open trash can but she didn't seem to care.

I left the Warden's office and roamed around till I found a tea stall. The stall served instant coffee, which I'm too much of a coffee snob to drink, so I ordered tea. I didn't want to occupy a seat in the tables near the stall that seated four to five people each, so I walked to the nearby park to sit at one of the benches, scribble in my notebook, and drink tea in peace, alone.

I considered changing hostels, but it didn't make sense to go to the other hostels if it meant I'd have a roommate. I'd rather live alone than live well. The last thing they can take from me will be my privacy, the little that I have in 216. I simply can't spend every second of my life worrying about my roommate finding out that I'm a lesbian. I'm paranoid as it is. With a roommate, I won't be able to talk freely on the phone or write what I want to without the fear of being outed. I've met homophobia enough times to know I won't love it.

Back when I started my relationship with Bhavya, I wasn't aware how rampant homophobia was. I used to come out to anyone without worrying what they'd have to say. I met homophobes soon enough.

Once at the end of Fencing class, I said to my teacher, 'I have to leave Fencing class early to go to an art exhibit.'

'Till when is the art exhibit? Will you be late coming back?' she asked even as she taught me how to parry with an Epee sword.

'Yeah, I'll be back by eleven, I think,' I said, preparing for a lecture about the dangers of girls staying out too late.

'Be careful,' she said. 'There are dangerous people outside the Andheri railway station after 10:30pm. Even men should be scared to be there that late.'

'Why?'

'My husband told me that there were flocks of gay men roaming outside Andheri railway station trying to meet other men for sex. It's not safe.'

'But I'm a woman—' said I, presenting, as it were, a weak defence.

'They'll grab you also,' she said. 'You don't know these men, what they'll do. They dress like women and beg on the streets but they are really men.'

After a moment's pause, she sighed and said, 'I don't understand why people want to be gay!'

Then she went on to explain how she was a counseller in a college in Bandra and how a boy in the college was gay and was teased for it. She said, 'I told him to cut his hair. Why does he have long hair when he knows it would make him gay? He even moves his hips when he walks like girls with long hair.'

I nodded as she went on, awkwardly parrying her opinions with my sword.

'Why would anyone want to be gay when they can just cut their hair?'

I waited as she searched her phone for a picture of the boy, wondering why she had a picture of the boy. I didn't confront the homophobe. I didn't say anything. Maybe I was too taken aback, baffled, speechless. I had no idea people were capable of such thoughts. Maybe I didn't confront her because I was a coward. I feel so much shame when I remember that conversation. Every time someone calls me brave for coming out, I think of this woman talking nonsense and how I didn't stop her.

A few months after this incident, I met a psychiatrist when I was getting tested for dyslexia. He worked at the best psychiatric facility in a public hospital in Bombay which was one of the two public hospitals that could officially diagnose dyslexia in the city. His job was to judge if I had psychological issues that would make me want to fake dyslexia for attention. It made me wonder if I *was* really faking dyslexia for attention, so to find out, I was completely honest with him about everything. But the minute I mentioned homosexuailty, he spent the entire hour asking me questions about my sexuality. I told him I had a girlfriend and he psychoanalysed me using Sigmund Freud's outdated theories.

'Who is the man in your relationship?' He asked.

'No man, we are two women,' I said. I genuinely didn't know some people asked this question about same-sex relationships till he asked it.

'No, no, I know, but who acts like the man?'

'No one,' I said.

'I mean, who initiates sex?'

'Sometimes I do, sometimes she does.'

He was visibly frustrated that he wasn't able to ascertain if I was the man in the relationship or not.

'When you go to a temple, do you visualise yourself having sex with the idols?'

'I haven't gone to a temple in the last five years.'

He kept asking irrelevant questions and got frustrated when I wouldn't give him straight answers. He concluded that I was a lesbian because I hated my father. Or was it that I hated my father because

I was a lesbian? I don't remember. He told my mother that I suffered from general anxiety disorder, bruxism, and clinical depression. He told her I was suicidal and she scolded me for it. She was angry that I had told him about our domestic situation. She said I couldn't commit suicide as long as I was living in her house.

I couldn't get myself to trust psychiatrists and counsellors after that. But I thought I could tell friends who have known me for years. Surely, they'll understand. I was visiting Delhi and staying with Preeti, a childhood friend of mine from the four years I went to high school in Delhi. She kept asking me about boyfriends so I told her I had a girlfriend. She was surprised and asked me if I was joking. When I showed her a picture of my girlfriend, she smiled and didn't say anything. We continued talking about other things before we fell asleep.

The next day we went to Connaught Place to meet Jayashree, another friend from school. Outside a cafe, we were taking pictures to post on Facebook. Jayashree was taking a picture when she noticed Preeti was standing at least two feet away from me. She asked us to stand closer and for Preeti to put her arm around me. I watched Preeti awkwardly considering if she should put her arm around me or not. I saw her lift her hand up and put it back down, trembling in indecision. At that moment, I knew. I knew that I was not one of them. I was different. Touching me was something she had to think about and consider. I was no longer a friend. Or a person. It was as if she wasn't sure how I'd react to her touch and she was too afraid to find out. She no longer knew who I was. I was just too different.

Given my previous experiences with homophobia, and given that it was 2016 when I was replaying these instances in my mind and it was still illegal to be in same-sex relationships as per the law of the land, I did not feel too confident that a roommate would react in an accepting and mature way. She'd probably interpret all my gestures sexually or report me and I'd get thrown out like that girl with 'homosexual tendencies' who made it to the newspaper. I decided I'd rather stay alone in my dingy hostel than have a roommate in a better one. My loneliness was not a choice, it was a necessity.

I think over the past few years, I've developed a sort of phobia of homophobes. A homophobeophobia. I'm afraid anyone I interact with could be a homophobe—strangers, old friends, acquaintances, cousins, distant relatives. So I can't be bothered to make an effort with any of them. Because eventually they'll ask me who I'm dating or when I'll get married and I'd have to lie to them. And if I have to lie to them about who I am, then why bother talking to them? I know telling people about my sexuality puts me in a dangerous position and it is in no way the same thing as my mother hiding my father's alcoholism and abuse, but I can't help feeling like I am my mother when I lie about myself. I hate it.

I hate silently listening to homophobic remarks and sometimes involuntarily nodding my head just to be polite. My entire childhood, I've played the conflict de-escalator in my family; my entire life I've trained myself not to get worked up, not to throw a punch—I can't punch homophobes now! And I'd rather not make a connection with someone lest I hate myself for listening to them bad mouth my community.

I left the park bench to go on foot and explore a small portion of the sprawling 2000-acre campus, determined to find at least one positive thing that I'd enjoy about the place. After thinking hard, I figured I'd probably enjoy the idea of staying in a *women's* hostel. I've never seen women move so freely; in the few moments I spent in the hostel, I saw a woman braiding her hair, another stepping out of the shower wrapped in a towel, another ringing the prayer bell and chanting a *shlok*, another eating directly out of a rice cooker, and yet another practising a *Bharatanatyam* sequence. There was something mesmerising about how free women are when men aren't around. I've never been in a public place without men before. I look forward to not worrying about inviting sexual attention for wearing short shorts or spreading my legs too wide or roaming about in a t-shirt without a bra. This is how being in public *should* feel like to a woman.

I wish I could live in a lesbian commune run by a matriarch. I visualise this long lunch table full of women talking about ideas, theories, and emotions, eating from a spread of dishes from different regional cuisines. I dream of a space filled with women writing poetry, drawing portraits, drinking tea, dancing, playing the *veena*, growing herbs, making furniture, doing yoga, bathing, soaking. We'd design a world for women where nothing would weigh more than what we could carry and nothing was out of reach for us. It would have jar lids engineered to slide open with a push from a woman's delicate hands. Nobody would tell us we need a man to help us navigate this world made for women. We could design women-friendly chairs, pants and bicycles.

Has any woman ever enjoyed riding a bicycle? Bicycle saddles irritate my vulva. A side effect of using something made by a man for men. When patriarchs *allowed* women to ride bicycles, we got the same seat with a set of narrower wheels. A structurally weaker bicycle for the weaker sex. How can the same saddle be comfortable for both sexes when our genitals can't be more different? No wonder many women don't ride bicycles and never develop the visual-spatial skills useful for driving other vehicles. It's all a plot to keep women from being truly mobile. This helps patriarchs take vehicular control from women by calling them terrible drivers.

Of course, women are terrible drivers. So many women learn how to drive a car in their late-twenties or thirties without ever having driven a cycle or a scooter. I'd be terrible at anything I start doing so late in my life, and I bet many men would be too if it happened to them. In contrast, men are encouraged to drive, and are given vehicles when they are young.

How can we compare driving skills between men and women when men have had decades of a head start over women? It's insane.

I often wonder how the world would have turned out if women were the ruling sex. I don't think we would have mined for coal, drilled for oil or fought physically violent wars—all virile affairs that have made the world what it is. When I make this argument, many men and women tell me that Margaret Thatcher and Indira Gandhi were women rulers who led atrocious wars. But women being the ruling sex and a woman ruling in a patriarchal society are very different scenarios. Even if Indira Gandhi was the prime minister, she had to appease her political party which was mostly full of men. She had to prove that she didn't possess the *weaknesses* they attribute to women, like softness and compassion. She probably had to overcompensate by showing toughness to be taken seriously. I actually don't know what a woman's world would be like. It blows my mind to even think of a world without wars and oil. Not that a woman's world would necessarily be a better one—it just won't be about physicality and brute force.

I should write a story about this.

6. Settling

Still day 1, It's almost 5 pm. Gloria from 215 said hi to me. She was at the University studying Theatre. She had short curly hair with bright pink highlights that looked really good on her. We chatted as her mother carried a single mattress up the stairs. I offered to help her mother, but she refused. Gloria offered me a can of diet coke that I refused.

'Do you smoke?' She whispered when her mother was far from us.

'Yeah, sometimes.'

'I also smoke sometimes,' she said.

'Have you met your roommate?'

'My roommate is a girl from MFA Painting. She finished her admission work, but she is staying with her father in a hotel this entire week.'

On seeing the mattress, I remembered that I'd also need one in my room. Gloria told me that she got a message from her friends about a second-hand mattress salesman who was selling mattresses to new joiners outside the ladies' hostel today. She told me to rush to him to buy one before he runs out.

The second-hand mattress was more like a stuffed sack. The salesman was also selling pillows but I thought I'd rather get new ones from the mall. I deserve one piece of luxury at least. I carried the heavy mattress to the first floor; my fingers could barely hold on to it. I had bitten my nails too short making the skin around the nails sore. And dysgraphia made my grip weak and my hands hurt from lifting for a few minutes. I could feel the mattress slipping out of my hands and I clenched it tighter, hurrying to my room. I dropped the mattress, half on the bed, half on the dirty floor. I wrestled it up and covered it with a king-sized bed sheet. I used one of my dysgraphia hacks: making the bed requires fine motor skills, but you can tie a king-sized bed sheet into a knot around a single mattress even with crippled fine motor skills. I tied two tight knots to keep the bedsheet in place.

I went back to Gloria's room; her mother was

just leaving. She gave me a hug and told me to help Gloria. I nodded and thought, 'What help am I?'

When her mother left, Gloria lit a cigarette and offered me one too. I was probably smoking after three months; the last time had been with my flatmate in Ahmedabad the day she moved out. My way of staying out of the habit is to never buy cigarettes and always borrow them from others. I always paid them back by buying them food.

It was dinner time at the mess hall. I had skipped lunch to wait at the Warden's room to get the single room. I was starving.

'Do you want to go to the mess hall now or later?' I asked Gloria.

'I can't eat that garbage, nobody does,' she said. 'There are three food joints on the campus that serve better food, or you can go outside the campus to a restaurant. A few of my seniors from my Bachelor's college are taking me out to a restaurant in some time.'

'Can I come with you?' I asked, hoping to have the cheapest dish at the restaurant.

'Do you have a ride? Or a guy who can give you a ride?'

'No, my scooter won't get here for another week.'

'Don't worry, we'll pack some food for you. What will you have, chicken or beef biryani?' She asked.

'I am a vegetarian.'

She looked at me, shocked. I was used to that.

'Just today or every day?'

'Every day.'

'Religious reasons?' She asked.

'No, I just don't like the taste of non-veg food,' I said. This was the truth. Eating off bones freaks me out for some reason. So I tried eating boneless chicken and didn't like the texture. Perhaps it was my Brahmin upbringing, perhaps it was just me—but unlike typical Brahmins, I don't care when others eat chicken, fish, beef, pork or anything else next to me. My brother is a non-vegetarian, my ex was one too—I never cared.

'You just haven't had the right kind of non-veg food,' Gloria said.

'Maybe.'

'You have to have non-veg food in Goa,' she said, 'It's delicious! Come to my house during the winter break and I'll make you eat yummy non-veg food.'

As unappetising as the offer sounded to my vegetarian taste buds, at least I'd have somewhere to be during the winter break that wasn't my parents' house or this hostel.

We talked about the non-veg food I could try and the restaurants I had to try them in. Even though being a vegetarian was not a big part of my life, I could tell that being a non-vegetarian was a big part of hers. She was already losing interest in our friendship because of it. I smoked another cigarette while she fixed her hair and make-up. She left with her seniors. By that time the mess had closed. I returned to my room, hoping I had packed biscuits—I hadn't.

I didn't have drinking water either so I stepped out with an empty bottle in my hand. I met Saisree outside who figured I was going to get water and started giving me directions to the nearest water cooler, which my dyslexic brain couldn't understand. I just nodded—I didn't mind the thought of getting lost and roaming around the hostel for a bit, but Saisree was kind enough to give me some drinking water from her stash.

She had already met everybody in our wing; she started telling me about them. 217 hosted two girls from Orissa studying Chemistry. 219 hosted two from Bihar; one studied Economics and the other, Philosophy. 220 hosted four girls from Nagaland whose subjects she couldn't discern from talking to them. Saisree told me the names of the girls in 217, 219, and 220, but I don't remember them now. My brand of dyslexia makes me forget names and faces. At this point, I was trying really hard to not forget Saisree and Gloria's faces. It was going to be a nightmare in a few months when I'd be walking across the campus and have students smile at me or greet me, with me wondering who the fuck they were.

*

I can't sleep. Don't know if it's the unfamiliar place or the uncomfortable mattress or the empty stomach. My mind is racing. I feel restless; I feel like running away. The sound of stray dogs barking puts enough fear in my system to paralyse my legs. I'm in bed, dead awake, having already read all the news stories on my phone three times. I'm tempted to log back into social media to distract myself, but I know it would be a painful distraction. The moment I am on social media, I'd want to check my ex-girlfriend Bhavya's account. She never posts anything, so checking her account feels all the more pathetic. I can't help but still care about her and it manifests as an urge to check up on her unobtrusively through social media. I've dodged the Zuckerberg rabbit holes for months now, and my mental health is better because of it. If I give in today, I know I'll check up on everyone from my past, compare my situation with theirs and feel bad. I need to stay away.

So instead, I lie awake at 3 am wondering if I'd take Bhavya back if she wanted to get back together with me. Like she'd want to. I probably won't want to tomorrow, but I'm pathetic at 3 in the morning. Even if she wants to be with me again, we can't exactly start afresh. We'd still have to sort through our problems and I don't think we'd be able to. We already tried for months but we couldn't.

Our relationship was great the first two years—we laid our souls bare, felt safe, and helped each other survive. Then her mother found out about us and asked her to break up with me. She did, but we couldn't stay apart. We got back together in a few hours. Our relationship changed though. For Bhavya, every moment she spent with me were moments she spent betraying her mother. She felt so much guilt and shame, it drew us apart. But we needed each other, so we stayed together another year, even though it wasn't working. I kept hoping she'd patch things up with her mother and we'd go back to the way we were. She kept hoping she'd get busy enough with life that it won't hurt her too much to dump me. She won: studying MBA in Ahmedabad distracted her successfully. Or I was the distraction that she couldn't afford anymore. She ended a three-year relationship on a phone call after I moved to Ahmedabad to be in the same city as her.

She just called one night and said, 'I don't think about you anymore.'

I've over-analysed what she meant by that so much that the words have lost all meaning for me. I still secretly hope she's less busy and misses me. Enough to call me to ask if we could get back together. But should I be with someone who didn't have the courage to be herself when her mother opposed it? Someone who ended a three-year relationship on a phone call when we could have easily met. Someone who never cared enough to check up on me after the break up. I deserve better. I deserve the stability of being loved by someone who wants to be with me no matter how inconvenient.

But who am I going to find? My ex was one of the few people I know who was a woman who liked a woman. (I don't want to label her wrongly;

she could be dating men for all I know) The last year with her, I thought: It was either this or being alone. Being alone is fine, but in my life, being alone means no close friends, no family, just me, and being *that* alone terrifies me. I wish I didn't feel so lonely.

But no matter how it ended, and how it was, I'm glad it happened. I keep imagining my life if it hadn't. I'd probably pretend to like boys like I did as a teenager. I was probably lonely enough to try and date a boy even if I didn't feel strongly enough. Our sexual incompatibility would have scarred both me and the poor boy. My first queer relationship was flawed, but no matter how flawed it was, it was better than me forcing a straight relationship. That's a sad filter on reality.

The power went off. There are no power cuts in Bombay and Ahmedabad, so I was facing a power cut after eight years. I didn't have candles or enough battery in my phone. I sat in the darkness feeling my sweat soak through and soil the new-old mattress. Gloria came back from the restaurant, straight to my room. We smoked a few cigarettes while she complained about how annoying her seniors were. It saved me, helped me take my mind off Bhavya.

The power came back after two hours and I finally slept at 6 am.

*

Day 2. I left my room to brush my teeth when I saw a note stuck to my door that said: *Please no smoke here. We are sleeping.* I knew I shouldn't have smoked that late in the night, but Gloria had already lit one; I thought the damage was done anyway. I was worried that Saisree or my other dozen neighbours thought badly of me for smoking. I can't afford to alienate them or have them complain about me.

I should stop smoking already. I had my first cigarette when I was 18. No peer pressure involved, I smoked my first few dozen cigarettes alone—mouth-fagged them cause I didn't know how to smoke. They were stale too, bummed from my father's old stash. My father always hoarded 20–30 cigarette packs in his closet drawer. His brand of obsessive compulsive disorder made him leave the first and last two cigarettes in each pack which he said brought him 'bad luck'. So I could smoke those 40–60 cigarettes for free, and I probably did.

I started smoking because I thought if I was addicted to cigarettes, the urge to smoke would be a strong enough reason for me to want to get out of bed every morning. For me, cigarettes wouldn't shorten my lifespan; they'd make me live longer than I wanted to. But I never really got that addicted to cigarettes. I've gone from smoking 30 cigarettes a night to zero for months without the urge to smoke. But I always got hooked again around exam time when the stress would induce frequent bowel movements that the cigarettes helped me suppress. I can see how smoking can be really useful in this hostel, especially to avoid using the hostel toilet too often around exams. Just have to smoke outside my room, probably on the hostel terrace.

I went to the washbasin to brush my teeth. I saw Gloria there shaving her legs, a heel pressed against the wall, razor in one hand and diet coke in another. The moment she saw me, she said, 'I bought six litres of diet coke last night. You can have as much as you like.'

'Why so much?'

'Water tastes weird.'

I immediately thought of Jaundice and Cholera. I asked, 'Do you mean water in the university or water in general?'

'Water in general.'

I told her about the note and she said, 'Saisree already complained to the warden about my smoking. I don't care, I'll smoke wherever I want. It's my room!'

'I'm just saying maybe we shouldn't do it after 10 in the night,' I said.

'Yeah. You know, I saw this really cute boy yesterday in the university,' she said.

'Oh—'

'Are you in a relationship?'

'No,' I said, 'but I got out of a long-term one recently.'

Recently? It's been a year.

'What happened?' She asked. 'Was he your friend from college?'

'Um—yeah.'

In the conversation that followed, she asked me which college I did my Bachelor's from, and I said Mithibai College in Bombay since I had already claimed to have met my 'boyfriend' in college; it would have been weird if I said I got my Bachelor's degree through distance mode after failing out of the degree I started at Mithibai College.

She asked me questions about my boyfriend, including his name which I told her was Bhavyesh.

I'm embarrassed I didn't tell her my ex was a girl. Sometimes it feels like talking about boys makes it easier to sustain female friendships. When I was in my teens, I never had crushes on boys so the girls didn't like talking to me. They probably thought I was a prude and if they talked about boys around me, I'd complain to their parents. Girls made fun of my prudishness. They'd ask me questions like what a romantic date was and laugh at me when I didn't know. By the time I was 13 and moved to Delhi, I figured that I just had to invent crushes to survive a teenage girl friendship. My first crush was a quiet boy in class. I like quiet people and I thought it was harmless, but they started teasing the poor boy with me. To stop that, I invented a boyfriend who went to another school. Our meet-cute story involved him crashing his bicycle into mine on my way to tuition. But all that while, I knew I didn't have crushes on boys and I felt alienated from a group of girls obsessing over boys. Like I felt alienated from Gloria now when she talked about her boyfriend and mine. I spent the morning hanging out in Gloria's room. Around noon, she left the hostel to meet her seniors. Having missed lunch time again, I went back to my room and laid down.

*

My loneliness is making me sick to my stomach. I'm restless, but I can't get out of bed. My stomach groans loudly like it is announcing its intention to devour me and put an end to the misery. Tears tease my eyes.

I am so fragile. I fall apart so easily. Nothing bad happened to me today. I was just lying down in silence when the panic attack came on. Now I feel like I am free-falling, waiting for the dramatic *thud*. I willed myself out of bed to get a smoke. I walked in the drizzling rain for twenty minutes to get to the university gate. I bought a cigarette and sat on a concrete slab near a tea stall outside the gate. There were groups of students laughing and eating around me. I should eat too. Maybe when my stomach stops growling, I will eat something. For now, I just sit inhaling smoke. It is a cloudy day, and the leaves wiggle on their branches.

I see an abandoned cart full of advertisement bills for personal loans and jobs. I wonder if I should post one: Are you free-falling too? Shuddering, awaiting the loud *thud*? Join me and we won't be alone, at least. What if there is someone else feeling the same way right now? It would be beautiful if we met. I wonder why I often feel like I am falling. Did nobody want to hold me?

There are people here whose eyes rest on me for a second. I see no pain in their eyes. They live so lightly; I wonder if they have ever fallen apart. My family never understood how I could get depressed without a trigger. There were days when I functioned only at a physical level, my emotions and my psyche weighted down by grief. People would ask me what was the matter, and I'd say nothing. They would have the most puzzled look in their eyes, as if it is not possible to feel grief from nothing.

Those who had a stable childhood can easily believe that everything will be fine. For them something going wrong is an exception to the normalcy of everything being fine. But when you come from a broken, abusive home, an uneventful night is an exception, and you expect things to go back to being terrible. When you are from a broken home, happiness can only be a soap bubble in a heat wave. When things are terrible, I'm busy suppressing my emotions and putting on a brave face so I don't get hurt. It's only when things are fine that I have the space to feel the bad times. So while 'nothing was the matter', I could still weep through the night like I'd lost a loved one. I was crying for the times I couldn't cry, when I didn't know the extent of what was happening to me. I was also crying to empty myself of grief on a quiet night so I could be fresh and ready to face more grief that I knew was coming.

I wonder how many years will go by till I am all cried out.

I grew up wondering how my parents never suffered mentally. After a night of fighting, even if the intensity of the fight was the same as every other night of that year, I'd still shut myself up and wallow. My parents woke up the next day brimming with hope and positivity. They'd go through the day pumped up and have energy left to fight again. Why did I suffer and why didn't they suffer? Why was I sleepless at night? Why couldn't I get out of bed in the morning? Why did I feel like crying all the time?

I think it's because they let it out and I didn't. They suffered trauma and transferred it to someone else. They continued the cycle of violence, purging themselves clean by lashing out. That's why they didn't think what they were doing was a big deal. They suffered, but they were fine. This cycle of violence stops with me. Or it goes into an infinite loop within me, into self-harm. I won't perpetuate it. If I do nothing else with my life, at least I can say that I took a lot of violence with me when I died. That's a lot of violence that won't multiply anymore.

Maybe that's why I like to write. It's a way to channel the violence and trauma out of me in small doses. I write about dysfunctional families, and I feel lighter. I write about trauma and when a friend reads it, we talk about it and it makes me feel better to some degree. I never felt seen before I saw *Who's Afraid of Virginia Woolf*. That film was about my family. Elizabeth Taylor played my father, insulting everyone, instigating fights. My brother and I were the awkward guests trying to escape. Watching it made me feel like I wasn't alone.

7. Working Out

❁

It's still day two. I managed to get to the mess hall on time for dinner. It took me hours of concentrating to accomplish it. My brand of dyslexia makes me tardy; I always forget what time I am supposed to get to places. Was it six or seven or was it eight-thirty? Time is a number, and I can't remember numbers.

Time is also a direction and I'm bad at directions. I can't remember which direction is clockwise and which is anti-clockwise. So I often read the analog clock in the anti-clockwise direction. Ten o'clock looks like two o' clock to me. My brother who is also dyslexic can tell which direction is clockwise but can't tell left from right. No two dyslexics are the same.

A digital clock doesn't help either, I get confused between the 12-hour and the 24-hour format. Once I was going to meet a friend at 1:30 pm for lunch. When it was 12:30 pm, I thought I had two hours to go: in my head the clock goes from 12:30 to 00:30 to 01:30. If I have to be somewhere at 2 pm and it's 1:50 pm, I might think I have 50 more minutes till 2. I forget that an hour has 60 minutes and always think it has 100 minutes. There's just something about time that I can't grasp.

It helps to set alarms, but there is always a chance that I'd get the time mixed up and set the alarm for the wrong time. Like setting an alarm for 3:40 when I wanted to set it for 4:30. There is also the risk that I'll snooze the alarm and forget or I'll leave the phone in the room and wander about, losing track of time. But tonight, I set alarms and asked Nita, my neighbour from Room 217, to verify them. She also told me the lunch and dinner timings and I wrote them on the wall of my room with a pencil. It made Nita laugh. I told her I was bad with time, and she said she'd remind me to go to the mess when she goes. How nice of her!

I'm prompted to eat only when I am hungry and I don't have military clockwork hunger that switches on at the same time every day. I don't think I'd be able to eat at scheduled timings. I am an individual. I want to eat when I am individually hungry. I am not fond of communal eating. The mess hall was scary today. There were about 70 people sitting close together and eating in one room, it was bizarre. I stood in a queue to get a plate, and then in another queue to get a serving of mushy vegetables. There was another queue for servings of rice, and another for gravy. It took me 20 minutes to gather my food. Did our stone-age ancestors spend so much time gathering berries in the wild?

I'd gladly eat berries than what was served in the mess. Liquid mush of different colours flow over each other without mixing. These liquids just float on top of the rice, in their order of density. The liquids were different colours but they all tasted the same bland. I took another serving of curd-rice; at least that's *supposed* to be bland. The curd was so watered-down, however, that it danced around the plate every time the wobbly table came into contact with one of the 70 women eating around it. It was unnerving.

I saw Saisree on my way back to my room and asked her if the mess food was always so unappetising.

She nodded and told me to try the North mess hall. I found out from her that there were two mess halls in our cluster of hostels: North and South. North wasn't a direction, but 'North' represented the food preference of North Indians, and the 'South' mess was for South Indians. The main difference was that the North mess served *chapatis* at dinner instead of rice. I thought *chapatis* would be healthier for me, but when I went to the mess the next day, they told me their mess was full.

*

Day five. My scooter was delivered today. Finally, I can be a bit mobile.

At the hostel, there have been several attempts at friendships. Who wouldn't want to be friends with this friendly face being nice to everyone so they don't complain to authorities about her if they find out she is queer. Saisree really wants to be my friend. Unlike her other friends, I had something to offer that she really needed. We are both fat girls, which automatically makes us weight-loss buddies. I was supposed to motivate her and talk to her about all the good times we'd have when we'd fit into retail clothing and find suitable bachelors to wed.

She had asked me if I wanted to go on a walk with her two times already. I'd turned her down those times, but when she asked today for the third time, it felt impolite to say no. I thought I could bore her or weird her out of the friendship. Maybe I could just show her my lack of dedication to get in shape. The walk started with us spending half an hour in her room with her friends discussing if it was too weird for her to walk wearing a t-shirt. It was no fancy t-shirt either, a one-size-for-all free t-shirt you get when you sign up to run a marathon. I asked her if she ran the marathon, and she told me her brother got it for working the sign-up booth.

'It fits weirdly around the breasts,' she said, arching her chest forward.

'No, it looks okay. Quite normal,' I said, nodding.

'It is weird.'

'Why wear your brother's t-shirt? Why don't you buy women's t-shirts? Maybe that'd fit better.' I said.

'Our village doesn't have stores that sell women's t-shirts.'

She went to the wash area and checked herself in the mirror. She said, 'There are boys from my village studying in the university. They'll make fun of me for wearing a t-shirt, I better change.' She wore a kurti instead.

Finally, we were out walking, and before she could say anything, I apologised for the cigarette smoke the other night. I am not proud of this, but I told her Gloria was the one who was smoking in my room, that she proceeded to smoke even though I'd told her not to. It is self-defence; I have to be in everyone's good books. Saisree was pleased to hear this. She asked me, 'What sort of woman would smoke? Why do people do it?'

I bit my lips and said, 'I have no idea why women would want to smoke.' I could taste the tobacco on my lips. I hate myself for this, but there is a lot of judgement around 'women who smoke' that I didn't want to attract. I like to mirror the person I'm talking to so nobody suspects that I'm any different from them. That way I 'fit in' perfectly in every group, and I can protect myself.

Saisree then asked me a lot of uncomfortable questions about my weight and my weight loss goals. She told me that she was doing a six-month weight loss programme and asked me if I wanted to join her. I think six-month weight loss programmes are great for people who are sure they'll live for six more months. I told her I didn't have the head space to commit. She looked disappointed. She complained a lot about her weight and the polycystic ovary disorder (PCOD) she had, which reminded me of my polycystic ovary syndrome (PCOS). I was worried again that my uterus was full of a hundred eggs that weren't breaking for some reason. I haven't menstruated once in the past two years. That can't be healthy. Or is it not *that* unhealthy? I can never tell. I've asked gynaecologists if it was terrible to skip a few months of menstruation if I didn't want to be a mother and they always say, 'You are saying you don't want to be a mother now, but you wait for a few years and that's all you want to be.'

They never answer my question.

When I was diagnosed with PCOS at 22, my gynaecologist referred me to an endocrinologist, and my mother and I visited him a week before I came out to her. He asked me to stand on the weighing scale and wrote down the number. He took out a measuring tape from his desk, measured my waist circumference and wrote down the number. As he wrote it, he said, 'You like potatoes and rice, don't you?'

He then wrote down numbers a healthy woman needs to be. Told me in great detail how far gone I was from the numbers I needed to be. He told me I had insulin resistance (IR), and that I should lose weight or he'll put me on diabetes medication. My life fell apart after that when I came out to my mother, and it didn't seem to matter that my numbers were wrong. I'd only binge-read about IR and PCOS anxiously a few times a year when I got worried about my health. I discovered that IR and PCOS were both metabolic conditions that promoted fat storage, especially abdominal fat. The way I understand it, the energy I was supposed to get from the food I ate instead got stored as fat so even if I ate the right amount of calories, it'd only make me grow tired and fat. The doctor made me feel like I had led myself astray from the 'right' numbers, like I'd convinced my organs to be insulin-resistant.

I would have never noticed that I was fat if people, like the endocrinologist, weren't constantly telling me. I always liked looking in the mirror; I always thought I was incredibly good-looking. I know I'm not conventionally beautiful, so to most people I'm probably ugly and undesirable. I just don't care about what such people thought of me. I have this weird unshakeable confidence about the way I look and the way I am. It didn't even matter to me when my classmates in high school in Delhi called me balloon or *moti*, the Hindi word for fatty. It only bothered me when I wondered if that was all they noticed about me. I told my mother about it, and she told me that she was bullied for being fat too and that it was normal for fat girls to be bullied.

My mother and grandmother kept shaming me for being fat, but never helped me eat better. Sometimes they even force-fed me a lot of food because we had leftovers and I was the only one in the house who complimented their cooking. They ate their feelings, and they taught me the same. I'm stuck in a cycle of corpulence, along with cycles of violence and anxiety. Some days I feel like I'm nothing but the intersection of these circles.

Regardless, I loved my body, still do. I think it's because of the confidence from getting a lot of attention when I was a toddler. I didn't have the brand of dyslexia associated with delayed speech. Growing up, I was the smartest baby in the family, memorising every song after hearing it once, getting perfect marks in my kindergarten exams, being well-behaved, saying smart things. I'm told I was humorous and witty too. I was celebrated as a prodigy. I started showing signs of dyslexia when I was 9 years old, in fourth standard, during my half-yearly exams. In my house, anything below a 100% in Mathematics tests was unacceptable. A score below 90% was tolerated because it was human to make silly mistakes. I had never scored below 80% till then but in that exam, I got 42%. We got the marks during parent-teacher day in school, an affair that was two hours long where my 59 classmates' parents tried to get the teacher to increase their kids' marks. My Maths teacher's table was packed but my mother sat on one of the two chairs near the teacher's table for an hour, completely shell-shocked that I'd scored below 80, that I scored below 60, that I scored in the 40s. She told me that I had left all the questions half-answered, which is a symptom of dyslexia but I'd only know that decades later. We left our Maths teacher's table to sit on a bench in the school grounds where my mother cried silently and pinched my thigh a hundred times. When I squeaked in pain, she pinched me harder and told me not to draw attention.

'I can't leave this bench,' she said. 'I can't go home and face our family who will blame me for your failure.'

My thighs were blood red, and in a few days, they'd be bruised black and purple.

A custody battle began at lunch. My grandmother, who used to be a Maths teacher, claimed that it was my mother's negligence that had caused my failure. She asked me if I preferred that she taught me instead of my mother. I said yes; having just been assaulted by my mother I thought my grandmother won't treat me *that* badly. But as I said yes, my mother was serving me *sambhar* and she got so angry with me that she poured piping hot *sambhar* on my bruised thighs. My thighs burned for days when my school uniform caressed them. I wanted to run away from home but I had nowhere to go.

I asked my mother about it a few years ago, 'How did you feel pinching me a hundred times that day?'

'I never did that,' she said. 'I might have hit you because I was upset that your grandmother was snatching you away from me, but I never pinched you. Do you know I was so sad that I went to Besant Nagar beach that evening and thought about drowning myself? You getting low marks meant I'd failed as a mother and I couldn't bear it.'

Anyway, that incident marked the end of my smart days. Every day after that was marred with beatings on the back, pinches on the shoulder or a whack on the back of my head. I was constantly told that I was stupid and lazy. My family thought I was wasting my potential and just the sight of me doing anything other than studying made them go mad with rage. I have suffered harsh beatings just for watching TV. I spent most of the day sitting in front of a textbook, crying. I spent my entire childhood willing myself to do what I was terrible at: recalling sentences exactly as they were in my textbook. And when I failed at it, I didn't know how to cope.

I stopped feeling my body to stop feeling the pain from the beatings. I remember hurting myself to train my body to feel numb to the pain my family inflicted on me. The only control they had over me was how much they could hurt me. I thought if I seized that from them by going numb to their beatings, they'd have nothing over me. I could finally do what I wanted and just take their beatings and continue to do what I wanted. Such were my dreams when I was 10.

My body changed when dyslexia kicked in. Before that as a prodigy I was used to a constant supply of attention and compliments. It was so long ago that I don't remember it, but I still feel it every time a family member who I haven't seen since childhood holds me in that high regard when they talk to me. My family lies to everyone about my academic performance so they don't know that I repeated a year in school or dropped out of multiple courses.

My weight is tied to my exams. I've gained five kilos for every exam I took. Some days when I'm stressing about exams, I'd give myself little treats, like a piece of chocolate, in exchange for studying for a few hours, like a dolphin doing tricks in the zoo. I started using junk food to make myself feel better, especially when I was nervous. I have memories of stuffing my face with food while staring into space, tense, thinking about all the beatings I'll receive when I fail an exam. I usually lost some of the weight, but I gained it back, exam after exam after exam, stress-eating, my legs shivering and my palms sweaty and cold from the fear of exams that always started the process of more hate and abuse in my household.

I used to get chills from anxiety on the morning of every exam. I've had teachers check on me, watching me shiver, and asking me if I should skip the test. There was no way I was going home without writing the exam and having my parents pound me, all hell breaking loose. I could get a stroke during an exam and the left side of my body would start drooping but I'd still be expected to finish the exam. It's Brahmin culture, after all.

I once saw a classmate have a seizure during an exam and I felt badly that he missed the exam. It made me worry how I could make my handwriting look legible if I ever had a seizure like that. I'd practise holding a pen and making seizure-like movements and writing, practising to make it legible. I couldn't have bad handwriting or I would have lost five marks.

I know I'll leave this university fatter than when I came here. Even though I barely eat anything at the mess, I know I'll start binge-eating packaged junk food soon. And I have come to terms with being fat. Who knows if I'd even live till the age when fat people get a heart attack? Sounds unlikely. Even if I did, I tell myself that being fat and dying from a heart attack earlier is a better way to go than dying of cancer, stroke, or dementia later. It's also the perfect metaphor, I tell myself, for my sad, lonely, and disappointing life—my heart giving up. Poetic, almost.

It's hard to make a connection between dyslexia and weight, but in my life, I know undiagnosed dyslexia has been a trigger for weight gain. I read online that there was research that showed that when dyslexia is untreated, it could increase the chances of anxiety, depression, and substance abuse in a person, and food is a substance. I remember gaining the first chunk of weight when I moved from Chennai to Bombay. When I was in Chennai, I was in an English-medium school with Tamil as my second language. When I moved to Bombay in the seventh standard, they only had Hindi and Marathi as second language options so I had to take Hindi. Usually, students with dyslexia were allowed to skip learning additional languages because learning to encode and decode in multiple languages can be a nightmare for a dyslexic brain. But in my case, I wasn't just learning three languages, I was learning three completely different scripts with no overlap. I was also learning Hindi alphabets while giving the same exam as my peers who already wrote essays in Hindi, who had studied the language five years longer than I had. That year, I lost interest in education. It was just too hard and I felt like a failure all the time.

I remember my parents tried to solve my Hindi problems by sending me to a lady for tuition classes. The lady already had 30 students of different ages and classes studying with her at the same time as she was trying to teach me Hindi from scratch. On the first day, she gave me the second standard Hindi textbook and asked me to read it in my head and let her know if there were words that I couldn't understand. I spent an hour sitting in a corner unable to read past the third word. When she asked if I had had issues, I said no, because I didn't know how to tell her about the issues I had—I couldn't express them. Since I had no issues, I was promoted to third standard and then to fourth standard. Fourth standard textbooks had stories instead of random sentences. They came with cartoons, which helped pass the time when I'd try to guess the story based on the cartoons to amuse myself.

The lady got suspicious when I told her I didn't have any issues reading the stories. She pointed at a word and asked me its meaning. I couldn't even read the word, so I had no idea. She told me the meaning and told me that I should ask her if I didn't know the meanings of words. So from then on, I pretended to read and then found random words whose meanings I could ask her to prove to her that I was reading. I started underlining words with more than four letters. I reasoned—longer words are harder. But those longer words turned out to be the name of a character in the story and I had underlined the same word eight times. She figured out that I couldn't read, and she didn't have time to teach me so she pretended like I was improving.

I failed that academic year. My family got so frustrated with me that I became their pinching bag. I must have gotten more than a few hundred pinches that year. A lot of whacks to the head and the back too, everybody in my house had a short temper. It was the same year where my only friend was an intellectually challenged girl who couldn't speak Hindi. The entire time I felt no different from her. It was the same year I tried to run away from home.

Imagine looking at words but not being able to read a sentence. Imagine reading a sentence and forgetting what you read immediately. Imagine reading half of one line and then half of another line. Imagine not being able to focus on a word so it looks like the letters are dancing. Imagine feeling so much shame for not being able to read that you fake an eye test to get glasses, then you break the glasses to tell the class that you don't have your glasses and that's why you can't read properly. Thank god my mother would rather I go blind than buy me another pair of glasses after I broke it in a week.

8. Unsettling

Day 7. I got my periods after not having had one for two years. My menses is a vindictive bitch to come now, when I'm trying to adjust to my surroundings, when I am trying to feel okay. I used to go to the toilet once a day, but now I can't help it. I woke up feeling a heavy flow coming down, and I rushed to the toilet which was occupied. I went to two other wings on the floor; all the toilets were occupied like they usually are till 9 am. I came back and waited, feeling my thigh getting wet. I hate rubbing blood off my underwear, it tires my fingers. I hate this.

I didn't want to go to the toilet every few hours, who knows what stenches, blood, and excreta would be left unflushed to greet me. I didn't know what else to do so I went to the mall to be able to use the mall toilet when I needed. There was a time when I used to think mall toilets were disgusting. But now I know better (or worse). I didn't want to spend the little money I had on a movie or food so I just sat in the food court watching people eat, waiting to go to the toilet again. After a while, my stomach cramps became unbearable, the way they do when I get periods after years of not having one. I wanted to lie down but I also didn't want to go back to the hostel. I let myself spend a little money and ate garlic bread. The carbs made me feel better enough to drive back to the hostel on my scooter.

*

I can't sleep. It's 4 am. I've been tossing and turning in bed since 10 pm. I fell asleep for a second and the sound of stray dogs barking woke me up. But I imagined that the dogs had busted open my door and were in my room (the door which I have lately managed to close to its hinges with a chair) and they were jumping up on me. I tried to move and get the dogs off me but I couldn't. I saw a feral dog sitting on my chest which felt really heavy. I kept trying to lift my hand, and suddenly I snapped out of it and into an empty room. I could move my hands again. A sleep paralysis episode. Is my sleep paralysis back?

I had my first sleep paralysis attack in Ahmedabad around Diwali when my flatmates were out of town. I slept alone and imagined an intruder breaking into my room when the sleep paralysis hit. I had an out-of-body experience where currents were passing through me and pushing me out of my body. I woke up panting, shit scared. I was so scared I called my mother who mumbled something and asked me to drink tea. I stayed up crying, feeling the spikes of adrenaline pulse through my body. I had no idea what sleep paralysis was till that day. I searched my symptoms online, and I spent the rest of the night reading about other sleep paralysis incidents and out-of-body experiences.

I'm too scared to sleep now. I want to go to the toilet but there were four stray dogs barking and squealing outside, growling at each other for leftover meat in the trash can. I'm still scared from the paralysis, and I still have my menses. I don't want to face those dogs smelling like anxiety and pheromones. Not like I can face those dogs even as my bravest self.

The dogs didn't leave for half an hour. Since I couldn't go to the toilet, I changed my sanitary pad in the room, standing up. I even washed my hands with drinking water after that, just let the water form a pool on the floor; I'll disinfect it in the morning. Or I'll forget I did that, slip, and break my hip. I really hope I don't start using my room as a toilet just because it's cleaner than the actual toilet.

Today, in the evening, I was on the phone with an old friend of mine, an ally. We were talking about loneliness and isolation. I was telling her how I feel being a lonely lesbian on campus. About ten minutes into the conversation, Nita from 217 knocked on the door and said, 'You know I can hear every single word you are saying?'

Now I am terrified. Does she know? Did I come out to her accidentally? Why else would she say she can hear 'every single word' that I was saying? How do I approach her and talk about this?

I slept again for half a minute and dreamt that there were campus authorities standing below my hostel room window with a megaphone shouting loudly, 'We know who you are. Pack up your things.' I've been wide awake since, talking to myself, cursing at myself for feeling free enough to talk so loudly in this room without walls and with a door that doesn't lock. I keep expecting the authorities to barge into the room and drag me out of the university. That would actually be better than the awkward dance I'm about to do around Nita wondering what she knows. No matter who she is, I have to befriend her now.

My nervous tics are back. Yesterday, I noticed that I've started hitting myself again. I enter the toilet hitting my head to distract myself from what I'd find, blood, feces or both. I can't even think about it right now without hitting myself. *Need to get this image out of my head. Need to get this image out of my head. Need to get this image out of my head.*

I think I am slipping again. I've started counting stairs, tiles, steps. I hold my fingers wide open, if my pointy finger touches the middle one by mistake, it has to touch all the other fingers the same way and repeat with the pointy finger on the other hand. I'm bothered by my toes scrunched together in my shoe, my eyeglasses touching my cheeks, the occasional hair on the back of my neck. I feel like pulling out my hair and cutting off my toes. I'm slipping.

My obsessive compulsive disorder (OCD) is back. I had full-blown OCD when I was young between ages 5 and 10 or so. The entire day I used to suck my thumb and touch my belly button with every finger one at a time and repeat. That was my favourite pastime. I used to eat in fours: four biscuits, four cups of peanuts, four everything. Once when I went to my friend's birthday party where my other friends and their parents were there, my friend's mother offered me a biscuit from a tray of biscuits and I turned her down. She asked me why I won't eat it, and I said I wasn't hungry. She insisted that I eat the biscuit so I took four biscuits from the tray. Everyone started laughing, because someone who wasn't hungry a second ago now wanted to eat four biscuits. I felt so much shame that day, I realised I had a problem. I didn't know it was called OCD till much later but I had seen the same patterns in my father.

My father always rang the bell two times. He'd get up from the chair, walk two steps, walk back two steps, sit in the chair again, and get up again. He'd slip his feet in the shoe, slip it out, and slip it in again every time he wore a shoe. He'd tie his laces, untie them, and tie them again. I knew if I continued eating in fours, I'd be doing everything my father was doing, but four times.

So when I was 9 or 10, I decided I needed to snap out of the habit. When I had the urge to eat four biscuits, I'd just block my thoughts and break a few biscuits and stuff them into my face without counting. When my thoughts were back, there was no way to know how many biscuits I ate so I couldn't be obsessive-compulsive about it. If my left hand touched a surface twice and I felt the urge to touch my right hand with it twice too, I'd block my thoughts and touch the surface with both my hands a random number of times so I couldn't keep score. I did that for years to snap out of my OCD. But sometimes when I'm anxious, I start counting things again and my OCD comes back. I have to keep blocking out my thoughts and introducing randomness in my routines to ward it off.

It's time for class, I haven't slept a wink.

*

Spotting a lizard near the bed in my room makes me squirm. I tried, I really tried to stay in the room and ignore it. But it was sprinting across the walls. I saw it swallow a bug and that made me cringe and gag. I tried to jam the room door as much as I could and left immediately. Not knowing where to go, I roamed the campus a bit, had a cup of tea, and came back to find the lizard inside the room, above the door. I quickly entered the room, got my laptop and glided out. Saisree saw me and looked puzzled. I told her that there was a lizard in my room. She nodded and told me that the lizard in her room sometimes wakes her up from sleep by making weird noises. She was talking about the lizard like it was her pet!

Nobody cared. I tried to tell other women about the scary lizard that sprints across walls and they behaved like it was nothing unusual. They even told me funny (scary) stories about the times lizards fell on them or into their food. A few admitted that they were scared of lizards but apparently not enough to abandon their rooms and want to burn the building down. Many showed me the lizards in their rooms, coolly hanging on their walls with their beady eyes vibing, 'I'm going to fall into your mouth while you sleep and choke you to death!' but others didn't get that vibe from lizards. For them it was a friendly old reptile that was nature's free bug repellent. Really?!

I spent the night on the floor of the computer room in my university department. A few classmates offered weed, but I refused. I am too paranoid now, weed will send me on a bad trip. And I didn't want company. I spent the night searching on the internet for nonviolent ways to shoo lizards. Apparently, there is a chalk-type thing that stops them from entering the room. It's funnily called *Lakshman Rekha*, which is a reference from Ramayana, a line that Lakshman drew on the floor to control his sister-in-law and restrict her freedom. I didn't get any sleep all night. When it was bright enough, I returned to my room, asked Saisree to help me get rid of the lizard. She laughed at me, but came to my room with a stick and poked the lizard till it ran out of the window. She saved my life.

I spent the rest of the day cutting open huge plastic bags and sticking them on the window and the open space above the door which was supposed to be a vent but it was half-closed with a piece of wood from the outside. Why did someone want to close the vent only half way?

I drove to the store and bought many products that kept lizards out including *Lakshman Rekha* and used it everywhere. I thought lines of *Lakshman Rekha* would cover all the mould, but the mould stuck to the chalk and soon I was drawing *Lakshman Rekha* lines covered in mould. Every time somebody closed their door in the wing, the air would be sucked out of the vent with a whoosh followed by a wheezing sound as if the air was being filled in and out of a plastic bag. It sounded like somebody was gasping for air. It was quite unpleasant.

I decided against the plastic bags and spent the day sticking layers of newspaper together to emulate the thickness of cardboard. I removed the plastic bag and stuck the newspaper on the door vent. I wanted natural light to enter the room so I didn't do that to the windows. Instead, I made makeshift window handles (all of them were broken) and shut the windows tightly. I turned the room upside down looking for other insects. Nope, just mould and ants now. I went to bed.

*

Day 10. Gloria is moving out of the hostel to a paying guest accommodation off-campus. The place, she showed me, was cheap enough and came with an attached bathroom, food, and laundry service. I was almost tempted to call my mother and negotiate with her to increase my allowance. Since I'm not lesbianing anyway, maybe I could tell her I won't lesbian for two years if she pays me more. But I don't want to deal with the awkwardness of mentioning my sexuality in front of my mother again. Staying off-campus is not worth the hassle of dealing with my mother.

And it's better this way. I'll get used to living like this: sharing a bathroom, giving up my privacy, being around stray dogs and lizards. Living off-campus is a quick fix for now but what after I fail the course and am jobless and broke again. The tiny allowance that I do get now is because I'm trying to get my life together and doing a Master's degree. I don't think my mother's generosity will continue if I fail again.

I helped Gloria pack, and all the while she was bitching about the hostel and calling it a filthy dump where she can't even smoke in peace. She is literally calling my house a filthy dump to my face with no regard for my feelings. I don't think I am going to miss her. I was already seeing the end of the friendship anyway; the last straw was when a few days ago she told me that gay people didn't exist because she didn't know one. I told her maybe she knows gay people but they just haven't told her they were gay. How brave of me to come out to her so slyly after telling her about my boyfriend named Bhavyesh. But I was right in not coming out to her, although my judgement these days warns against coming out to anyone. I'm too fragile.

*

Day 12. Got the first assignment of the semester today. I have to make a presentation about any recent news article. I love open-ended assignments so I've been excitedly looking at recent news articles and thinking about topics I want to present on. I'm interested in exploring fake news or maybe cryptocurrency. I haven't done a presentation in five years; my last time was in my school days. I've forgotten my coping mechanisms.

Public speaking can be challenging with dyslexia if it involves reading off a script. When I was in the 9th standard, I used to present class assignments extempore and I did it well enough to get selected to present at an international forum in the United States of America. But the stakes were high so I had to read off a script that my teachers wrote which they edited every week. I couldn't rote-learn it, and I couldn't read properly so I was always stammering, reading words wrong, skipping a line, pronouncing words wrong—the typical dyslexic reading, but I didn't know at that time that it was because of dyslexia.

My teachers used to scold me and threaten to cancel the trip if I didn't speak properly, but the tickets were already booked. I could see the regret in their faces for choosing me and I used to be really hard on myself, feel nervous as hell, and cry every day because I just couldn't read. It created a lack of trust in my own abilities because, to me, at that time, it seemed like I was both good at public speaking sometimes, and really bad at it at other times. I still don't trust my abilities. Even though my confidence made me sign up for things that were challenging, I could never trust myself to do anything properly.

But the whole experience has made me numb to humiliation which gives me a weird kind of courage to try things without the fear of making a fool of myself. I've already made a fool of myself—and survived. I've had a few hundred eyes on me while I watched my palms sweat and then grease the sheet of paper I was holding, as I read and reread and reread the same basic line to get all the words right. What can be worse than that?

9. Bathing

Week 2. Such water scarcity in this hostel; we don't have running tap water on most days. The others in my wing leave the taps open where there is no water and when we get water, the taps keep running and all the water goes down the drain. And others, Saisree especially, just leaves her bucket under the tap, opens it to full force and leaves to do other chores. I've become the self-appointed water police of the wing now, telling others to close the taps when I find their buckets overflowing. I hate myself for becoming *that* annoying bitch, but it really bothers me when someone wastes water.

Even if we get water for just two hours in the day, I'd like to know when those two hours are so I can have a tiny bit of control over my life—but no. Today I discovered that only my wing had a water issue. Other wings had water when we didn't. I've been going to the other hostel wings every time I want to use the toilet. Today I considered showering in the other wing's bathroom but couldn't get myself to. At least I'm sharing the bathroom with people I know here, who have now become familiar strangers. I don't know how I feel taking a shower in a bathroom used by total strangers. So I've been lugging a bucket full of water back and forth a couple of times and I realised, I have a weird showering ritual.

Whenever I'm about to take a shower, I fill the bucket with piping hot water and pour it on the floor, walls, pipes, and taps. Then I wear my slippers to step into the bathroom and keep wearing them as I shower. When I'm in the bathroom, I frantically pour water over myself from the bucket and scrub myself with soap as fast as I can, like it's a race against time before I catch something. Then, I wash my slippers and my bucket with piping hot water again. I try to sterilise the bathroom and then I sterilise everything I took to the bathroom before taking it back to my room. Today I had to do all the sterilisation by lugging buckets of piping hot water from the other wing, at least 30 feet away. All this when my flat feet could have easily caused me to trip, and my dysgraphia could have easily caused me to drop the bucket. Why am I not just taking a shower like everyone else here? Am I paranoid?

Something is wrong with me.

*

My nervous tics are getting worse. I have seen such nasty faeces and blood in the toilet and the bathroom, I get stressed just opening the toilet door. I'm hitting myself in the head harder every time to divert any attention from what I see. It's what I dream about too. I used to have these dreams where I would be stuck in a building. I would get into different elevators that went horizontal and vertical to different floors. Some won't move at all. I would spend hours in the building—in my dream—searching for the exit. I feel like I had the same hopeless dream last night. But I wasn't looking for an exit, just a clean toilet. All the nasty faeces in my dream, ahhhhh… the gag reflex woke me up. My head felt so sore, I was probably hitting myself in my dream too.

*

I figured a hack to fix my nervous tics. I noticed that the maid cleans the bathroom and toilet every day at one in the afternoon. I opted out of my afternoon class so I'm in the hostel during that time, so I can oversee the cleaning myself. I bought powerful bleach and cleaning supplies for her to use, but it wasn't very useful on stains that were older than I was. During the afternoon, everyone is usually in class or at the mess hall, there is barely anyone in the hostel. So as soon as the maid cleans the toilet, I use it. I take a shower right after that; being able to smell the traces of disinfectant puts a smile on my face.

I also figured a workaround for dealing with the water scarcity. It involves a posture where I stretch my hands out at an angle and tilt my hips in such a way that when I pour water from a mug, the water wets the maximum surface area of my body. When I bathe standing in such a posture, I can wash my hair and my body with a single bucket of water. That's down from the two and half buckets that I needed earlier. I don't have to travel back and forth many times to bring water to the bathroom in my wing, I only need to do it once. And once I'm done bathing I go back to the other wing to wash the bucket and my slippers—the only two things that came in contact with the bathroom floor. My bathing routine is more manageable now.

These hacks have really improved my mental health. But I wish I could get more accustomed to these things. It's silly and immature to be so squeamish. I wish there was a programme, something like stripping of privileges 101, or a self-help book, that would talk about how to get used to looking at other people's feces, blood, and vomit. I didn't plan on being so finicky. I didn't know that I was being brought up in a sheltered and privileged way till I was too old and accustomed to those things. I wish I wasn't.

Every time I feel like leaving this place, I wonder if it's because I'm spoiled or because I'm disabled. Is it my privilege or my mental illness that is urging me to leave? I wish I had people around me of one type or the other so I can at least share how I feel and introspect. I know I feel bewildered and crippled about facing everyday challenges. I just can't seem to ignore things that others don't even notice. I can sometimes smell the open garbage can in my room, and it smells so strong that I feel like the garbage can is actually inside my room.

I even notice sounds that others can't hear. Every once in a while, I can hear the sound of papers shuffling. Especially early in the morning when I'm sleeping. I can hear it so loud, I am woken up by the sound. I asked Nita what it was and she said she didn't hear it at all. It is a faint, soft sound, but it is so distinct to my ears. I wonder what it is. Am I going mad?

*

Today is a special day. I woke up to a power outage and there hasn't been electricity in the wires or water in the pipes for six hours. I have been lugging buckets full of water from the other block and throwing it in the toilet every time I need go. It's a good workout without the shower or the ceiling fan to cool me down.

When I complained to the warden about water shortage, she said, 'There is no such thing as continuous water supply during Indian summers.'

Every time I go to the other block with buckets to fill water, I feel like the women over there judge me. While I was there, filling my buckets, they came to the bathroom for their baths, or to apply make-up, or wash their feet, and they gave me such withering glances that I felt like the scum of the earth. As if I was there without any authority, without their consent, to steal their resources. They made me feel like I was polluting their precious bathroom with my unfettered greed. Like they were gods, casually roaming around while liquid gold flowed through their taps, like it was nothing. And I am an earthly scoundrel, who at the sight of liquid gold schemes to accumulate it and preserve it to feel equal to them.

As the day progresses, I can't help but feel like an inferior being who has failed. Failed to secure a running water connection in her own capacity. I don't have the guts to bathe in the bathroom in the other hostel wing either. What if the water runs out while I'm bathing? I can't ask strangers to hand me a bucket of water when it's their territory and I'm there without their consent. I already feel disgusted with myself for taking two full buckets from their bathroom.

When I brought the last bucket of water to my room, I stubbed my toe. A whole bucket of water splashed across the room on my shoes and my bag. I had class today. Guess I have to wear slippers to class. When I was leaving the room, I saw Saisree and her friends pack up and leave for their village. I was enraged. How dare they leave at this difficult time? It was especially in bad taste because I remember they were the ones washing clothes for four hours right before the water ran out.

Something has changed in the way I look at people now. My opinion of people used to be based on how genuine and sensible they were. These days I base my opinion on how careless they are about water. I like neighbours who spend less time in the shower. And really, which sensible person would waste water when there is a shortage? Which sensible person would invite people to stay over in their room when those of us who are already here don't have water for ourselves?

I'm starting to sound like an anti-immigrant nationalist. What is wrong with me? I'm talking about outside people using shared water that I'm entitled to like xenophobes and nationalists talk about immigrants taking their jobs. Maybe this is an opportunity to understand the anti-immigrant stance. In the hostel, the way I have seen water scarcity actually being a real thing, I wonder how many anti-immigrants have evidence of their resources being scarce. To me, it always looks like a political ploy to make resources appear scarce to enforce nationalist sentiments. This is interesting, maybe I could write a story about this.

*

A few weeks before the midterms and we have been getting more assignments. I usually sit aloof in the classroom, keeping only to myself. Why make friends I can't be out to? I don't particularly enjoy talking about Bhavyesh so much. And why make friends when I'll fail the course?

But we have assignments that we need to do as a group of two to four classmates, and I need a reliable person to do these assignments with since that really determines my chances of staying in the university. Half my class already know each other from their Bachelor's degree. And the other half have become friends with each other already based on ethnicity or shared interest. I want to find someone who is serious about doing the assignments well and who is easy to work with, without too many expectations from me of friendships and such. So I'm being friendlier with my classmates as I look for this person.

I invited a classmate to my room after meeting her in the mess hall. She is an outspoken ally; I asked her if she knows anyone queer and she said no. From experience I know this could mean she is anywhere between: an actual ally and a pretend-ally who kisses other girls for male attention. She seems smart though and doesn't talk much. We could make a good team and work on LGBTQ+ topics for assignments. I want to do a radio show about the transgender community in Hyderabad and she'd probably be onboard.

When she came to my room, she said she was surprised how different my hostel was from hers: how dirty it was, but also how nice it was that I had a single room. She sat on my bed, right on my pillow, and wrapped herself with my blanket. We talked for an hour, and the entire time I was really uncomfortable thinking: Why was she sitting on my pillow and touching my blanket? I kept thinking about how I was going to clean the pillow case, and how I haven't figured out how to wash clothes yet. When she left, I changed the pillow case and wrapped the blanket and put it away in a plastic bag. Why did I do that?

It reminded me of the time when my family lived in Delhi, and my father had a driver who used to sit on one of our two-seater sofas while he waited for my father to get ready for work. Sometimes, when my father ran late, he'd even lie down on the sofa and watch the cricket match that my grandfather was watching. This bothered everyone and caused a scandal in my house. My parents and grandparents would have elaborate discussions about why he felt the need to lie down on our sofa and what we were going to do about it. Finally, my grandfather told our driver to sit on the floor instead of the sofa. My grandmother refused to sit on the sofa again. She'd scold me and my brother if she found us sitting on it. Eventually, the sofa was tossed out.

I didn't understand the possible caste implications of the incident at that time. I was introduced to caste in school when I was 14. We were taught the names of the four castes, the term untouchability, and the names of revolutionary thinkers like Ambedkar and Periyar who were against the caste system. I remember coming home from school and asking my grandmother which caste we were. She said: Brahmin, of course. But it wasn't that obvious to me. In school, we were taught about the caste system like it was a thing of the past; much of the details of the history of caste discrimination were glossed over. I never thought of caste as something that had anything to do with the present or my life. In my mind, my knowledge of caste was filed alongside my knowledge of the Pythagoras theorem—something I wasn't sure why I needed to know.

So when the whole sofa situation and other similar situations happened, I didn't realise it was caste prejudice. I only discovered it was all caste prejudice three years ago, in Bombay, when my grandmother who could no longer walk because of being afflicted by Parkinson's disease was disgusted at being touched by her caretaker. She would make faces and throw temper tantrums when the caretaker used to feed her or help bathe her. One day, she started crying and wailing in Tamil that she didn't want to be touched by the dirty woman. I was shocked by her bigotry.

At that time, my grandmother was also diagnosed with early-onset dementia. Every time she didn't recognise me or forgot my name, I'd jokingly ask her the formula for tan(3θ) and when she got it right, I used to say that she loved Maths more than she loved me. After watching her lose her temper every time the caretaker touched her, I had to grapple with the realisation that her bigotry was perhaps stronger than her love too.

Growing up, I looked up to my grandmother. She and my grandfather actually had an equal and respectful relationship—and together they were the stable parental presence in my life. My grandmother was our household's matriarch, a staunch feminist. Even after my mother's family insisted, she refused my mother's dowry, which was still a rare thing in the 90s. She had a towering presence in our house, and I revered her discipline and sense of cleanliness so much, I had unconsciously modelled myself after her. I used to try to impress her by how thoroughly I could clean an old suitcase or my shoes. And I found no issue in the way she used to think, and I too divided the world into the clean and the dirty—and only a select few made the clean category. Soon, her way of thinking became a voice in my head:

'Can you smell that terrible stench in their house?'

'Her hair looks like a bird's nest!'

'These people don't bathe regularly.'

'Don't be friends with her, she probably has lice.'

'He got sick from his snot-nose friend.'

'Look at her filthy clothes. She was wearing the same thing yesterday.'

'This is not clean!'

'That is not clean!'

Since I didn't know much about caste—I just assumed everyone was dirty. I'm so pathetic to change the pillow case just because someone else sat on it. But every room I enter, my first thought is always about the stench or the dirt. It's the reason I can't be comfortable around anyone. Am I a bigot if I discriminate against everyone I don't personally know for no reason? Yes?

But am I a casteist person? I've always supported reservation, I think it's only fair if we have reservation for a few hundred years, at least. After all, Brahmins unofficially had a 100% reservation on education and jobs for a few hundred years. My grandparent's grandparents were educated. Both my grandfathers have Master's degrees. I clearly have a big advantage and a head-start over a first-generation college-going lower caste individual today. And I think lower caste people deserve more institutional empowerment than we have today—be it reservation, scholarships or other facilities.

Am I a bigot? Clearly, I was raised by bigots. Only a mentally ill person can think one person is intrinsically better than another. And I was conditioned by mentally ill people, like my parents were, like my grandparents were, to believe I was special just for being born in a Brahmin family—and others weren't. The ugly head of Brahminism cunningly hides behind the word hygiene. It's not hygiene, it's discrimination. I recognise that now. But how do I stop this voice in my head that tells me I have to clean everything someone touched. I have to slowly get myself out of this mindset and this hostel will help me with that.

There is hope for me because I did get out of the Brahmin mindset with regard to sex. When I think about how I came out to my mother, I think she was more disturbed that I had had pre-marital sex than that I had same-sex sex. Pre-marital sex is just not something good Brahmin girls from respectable families do. My mother probably thinks that as Brahmins we are only supposed to have sex to procreate, not to orgasm. Good Brahmin girls only had post-marital sex till they made two or three babies. I'm not a good Brahmin girl, I've had sex before marriage, and the kind that can't even make babies.

I often wondered how I had the courage to come out at 22 to my Brahmin mother at a time when homosexuality was illegal. I would have pegged myself to have suppressed my sexuality, had a husband and a child or two, and finally come out when I was 40 or 50. Or maybe I would have lived a lie, never owning my sexuality, just likc my mother or other women in my family might have done before me.

But I was saved because I discovered my clitoris when I was 10. One day, in the bathroom, the hand shower wandered to the sweet spot which when I caressed long enough suddenly sent a wave of delightful energy through me and made my feet feel cold on the floor. I loved how my mind felt afterwards, like it was wiped clean. I felt like I was reborn after every orgasm. It felt so good that soon enough I worried that it would give me cancer. So, I stopped messing around with my clitoris, from the fear of cancer.

I started giving my clitoris love again a few years later; I figured just because it felt good doesn't mean it was carcinogenic. But I didn't think I was doing anything sexual, that what I was experiencing was an orgasm. I thought it was pleasure like the one I got from hurting myself. Like when I pressed my fingernails on my gums really hard, or when I bit the skin around my nails. I always felt pain when I did these things, but it felt good too. For many years, I believed that the orgasm I experienced came from self-harm. And thank god, because if I had believed I was doing something sexual, I'd have stopped. I was repressed as hell at that time.

I only knew it was an orgasm at 18 when I discovered the word clitoris. I saw the word in an article about Female Genital Mutilation and looked it up. I knew about Female Genital Mutilation before I knew what a clitoris was, which is ridiculous. I wish the humble clitoris had gotten a shout-out in my science textbooks; it would have saved me years of worry about getting cancer. My science textbook did have a chapter about reproduction with a diagram of the female reproductive organs. But not a mention of the clitoris.

10. Doing Chores

❁

Week 3. I've decided to wash clothes today. It wasn't a difficult decision; I've nothing clean to wear. There are washing machines in the university, but it's on the other side of campus and the student to washing machine ratio is like a few thousand to one. There is usually a long line and I'd have to wait there for a few hours just to get my clothes washed. Nobody in my wing uses them, they wash clothes with their hands.

I have never washed clothes with my hands, apart from getting a few bloodstains off my underwear. I just figured out how to use a washing machine when I moved to Ahmedabad, and I've mostly been a disaster with it: forgetting to add detergent, leaving washed clothes in it overnight, adding so much detergent that the machine overflowed with soap foam. I used to despise the dull chore of getting the laundry out of the washing machine and hanging it all out on a clothesline to dry. I wonder how difficult and dull it's going to be to wash clothes with my bare hands.

YouTube wasn't much help so I asked Nita to show me how to wash clothes. And I'm taking notes. I need to fill a bucket with water and mix detergent in it. Then I add the clothes and, apparently, I have to let it soak in the bucket for an hour. While the clothes were soaking, Nita mimed the washing routine but she looked like she was doing a strange occult dance with a garment. She swirled it, scrubbed it, rubbed it, rinsed it, dipped it, squeezed it—I don't remember in what sequence. It looked too complicated for notes. I asked her if there was an easier way to do it. Nope. I asked if there was a way to wash clothes where I can stay dry through the process. She chuckled. She didn't understand why it mattered to be dry through the process. Why get wet and suffer from sinus the next day?

I have to wash the clothes. I *have* to. The clothes have been soaked for an hour and I asked Nita to watch me wash them and give me pointers for improvement. I stood by the washing counter, holding a drenched squiggly underwear of mine at a distance from my body. I squeezed the soapy water out of the garment. The entire time I was scared that the centuries-old water heater that was above my head would explode. I was also scared that a rat would emerge from the drain hole near my feet and run all over my body. I was not sure if I should lean forward to save my head from the heater or stand away to save my foot from the rat. So I stood away, leaned forward, and squeezed the garment, much to the amusement of any passers-by. Some even stopped what they were doing to watch me. I tried to squeeze the clothes harshly and got more chuckles. Apparently, I wasn't squeezing hard enough unless I applied my weight on the garment and got wet in the process. I did exactly that, but my spectators thought I still looked funny doing it.

Nobody believed it was my first time washing clothes by hand. Why would I need to when I grew up with maids and washing machines? I used to throw dirty clothes in the laundry basket and the clothes got clean somehow and showed up neatly folded in my organised closet days later.

My hands hurt so much from just washing four pieces of underwear. It's not privilege, or the lack of practice, I'm sure it is the dysgraphia. I called my brother who also had dysgraphia and asked him how he managed to wash clothes and stay sane. He said he loved washing clothes.

'How do you wash clothes?' I asked him, hoping to find a simpler process.

'Oh just soak your clothes in detergent water overnight, wring them, and set them out to dry,' he said.

'No. There is a lot of rubbing, squeezing, and dipping involved. How'd you get the detergent out of the clothes from just wringing them?'

'Don't add a lot of detergent and it comes off. All the other steps are optional, no?' he asked.

Still not sure if it is privilege or dysgraphia that has crippled us from washing our own clothes properly. I washed as many clothes as I needed for a week with as little rubbing as possible. Not super happy with the outcome but I got a week's time to figure out a way to do this.

*

These days it rains heavily during lunch and dinner hours. Even if I miraculously manage to remember the meal timings and to take an umbrella with me,

I still get wet and it triggers my sinus. Might make sense to invest in an electric cooker like the others have in the wing. That way I'll also not have to eat white rice twice a day and spike my insulin levels. White rice makes me sluggish and my insulin resistance means a lot of insulin just circulates in my blood and makes me feel hungry all the time. Coupled with the stress of exams, I'll be shopping for bigger pants. I need to break out of that cycle.

Cooking in the hostel room is against the rules and I could get caught, but I don't care. How can the university expect students from different parts of India with different dietary cultures to just eat white rice and mushy vegetables? How can a non-vegetarian realistically eat meat just once a week? No wonder Gloria never ate in the mess hall. It's casteist to pander to the preferences of the vegetarian upper caste when the majority of the people in India eat non-veg food. I don't mind rebelling against this by getting a rice cooker.

But the electricity is unreliable and my brand of dysgraphia makes it hard for me to cut vegetables. I chop them unevenly and get so tired doing it that I sometimes get frustrated before I'm finished cutting it all and throw away a few full brinjals or half an onion in the bin so I don't have to look at it again. I love eating Ivy Gourd, but when I cut it unevenly, half of it burns and the rest remains uncooked—and it looks ugly. I can't use sharp knives or I'd cut myself. A blunt knife will make me apply more pressure into the cutting and tire me faster. Everything is difficult.

Dyslexia makes me look stupid, but dysgraphia makes me look like a sloppy human being, almost like a toddler. Like a toddler I can't tie my own shoelaces so I've just learnt not to trip over them. I've gotten beatings from teachers in school for running around with my shoelaces untied. They thought I was unruly. I didn't know back then that some students had trouble tying shoe laces, so I didn't know how to explain the problems I faced tying them. Every time I'd tie them, they'd come untied in a few minutes. If an adult was kind enough to tie them for me, I never untied them. I just squeezed my feet into the shoes and pulled the heel counter from under my heel harshly till my face and fingers turned red. I don't remember who tied my shoe last, but I haven't untied them in three years.

I think dyslexia is a disability only in the context of a world that measures intelligence as the ability to read and memorise facts and spellings. Otherwise, I've loved having dyslexia and the roundabout way my brain works when I'm not stressing about exams. I think dysgraphia, especially motor dysgraphia that impairs fine motor skills, is a physical disability in all contexts. Fine motor skills are literally what makes humans different from chimpanzees. So many everyday tasks involve using fine motor skills; I don't know if I can ever live without someone's help.

But I look able-bodied to everyone. I have had people ridicule the way I hold a pen or a spoon, like those who ridiculed the way I was washing clothes. I wish people didn't assume everyone was able-bodied. There are so many who suffer from mental ailments, chronic pain, and diseases. I wish there was more awareness and compassion in the world for disabilities that aren't visually obvious.

I'm so used to people seeing me as able-bodied that I see myself as able-bodied too; I give myself a hard time when I can't do something that an able-bodied person can. I keep forgetting that I can't hold things in my hands for too long, I can't change bedsheets, I can't write for too long, I can't play musical instruments or video games for too long, I can't use a pen, spoon, knife, or pair of scissors properly.

*

I just saw a rat jump out from Nita's door vent onto my door vent. It created a paper shuffling sound as it ran into the space between the wooden block that half-shuts the vent from outside and the layers of paper that I had stuck on the inside of the vent. A rat was making that paper shuffling sound all these days!

I should have known this would happen. Of course, there is a rat in Nita's room; everything she owns is always on the floor—her books, her clothes, everything! Sometimes she would cook and leave vegetable peels and bowls of leftover food on the floor without cleaning it for days. This was easy access for the enterprising rat. I had an argument with her about this, and she refused to take any blame or responsibility for the rat infestation. According to her, she was also a victim of the rat which would have been there regardless of how she kept her room. But really, there is a specific reason the rat was inside her room of all rooms.

Ever since I found out about the rat in my vent, I keep imagining a hole in the layers of paper I stuck on the vent, and I panic that the rat is in my room. So I added more layers of newspaper to it. There go all my plans of befriending Nita. There is no coming back from calling a person responsible for a rat infestation. Guess I'll just wait for her to tell the authorities about my homosexuality and get thrown out. Just as well. It's better than living with a rat.

*

After my altercation with Nita, I'm realising how truly annoying she was. Her room was a dump. Every time she washed clothes, she'd wring them in the common area and make the floor wet; I almost fell so many times. The most annoying thing about her is the sound of her *payal*, the noisy anklet, that'd make the sound *kich, kich, kich* whenever she walked. I can't hear my own thoughts when she walks. And hate it more because the sound reminds me of Bhavya.

During the first year of my three-year relationship with Bhavya, I used to meet her almost every day. At 8 am, I used to drive 40 minutes on my scooter to sneak into her house after her parents left for work. She'd still be in bed, and we'd stay there till noon. I can still feel the rush I felt when she'd open the door for me; for a second I'd be awestruck by how breathtaking she looked. I'd try to kiss her, but she'd push me away so that I didn't smell her morning breath. She'd then brush her teeth while I held her from behind and kissed her neck till she dripped toothpaste on her pyjamas. We'd go kissing to the bed, undressing, caressing each other—and in a few hours we'd wonder where the time went.

One such day we were in bed, Bhavya sat up, went to her dresser, took her *payal* out, and wore it. She danced a *Bharatanatyam* sequence depicting Radha adorning herself to meet Lord Krishna. Her *mudras*, gestures, depicted a shy Radha looking in the mirror. Her dance showed graceful Radha doing *sringara*, wearing a *Nethi chutti*, and applying *Kungumam* on her forehead; Radha looked in the mirror for a moment, thought of her Krishna, and blushed. Bhavya blushed as Radha, and the way she blushed! I was amazed that I could make someone blush like that, I was moved to tears.

Bhavya continued dancing, gesturing to show Radha roaming the garden collecting flowers. A peacock danced and a deer galloped around Radha while she tied the flowers she had collected into a garland. Bhavya danced like Radha was dancing with the garland, and finally Bhavya walked up to me and gestured like she was putting the garland around my neck. She said, 'I now know *Sringara*.'

*

Still forgetting the lunch and dinner timings at the mess hall. By the time I ask someone, they tell me it has already closed. It is five in the evening and I have been starving the entire day. I wish I had bought chocolates at the store. All I had was whisky so I chugged a few pegs down. I heard Nita leaving her room as she talked on the phone. I had the sudden urge to follow Nita wherever she goes, if it meant that I'd get to the mess hall on time to eat the green mush for dinner. As I stepped out of my room, she turned back and looked at me worriedly, as if she had heard my thoughts.

I took peg-sized whisky bottles for the journey so I can pretend to throw a bottle at approaching stray dogs to scare them and protect myself. Nita hurried away so fast that I lost track of her before we even left the building. Committed to eating dinner, I went to the mess hall and climbed up to the terrace where I lay on the floor in the hope that

I'd hear the commotion of women heading to the hall when it opened. It was seven in the evening, the sky already dark. I saw the crescent moon slowly gain its lustre as the sky darkened. I wished I was with someone; we could have lain together on the terrace with our hands laced, watching the sky and feeling each other.

But the thought of lying in a public place with someone makes me feel uncomfortable. Maybe I won't care if I was with someone who didn't care; someone who made me feel safe outdoors. I've always felt vulnerable outdoors and even more so in the dark. I applaud women who feel at home after dark in public places. I wish I could be like them and reclaim the streets, the city, and the night. I wish I wasn't always associating the outdoors with sexual assault and rape. Screw all the men who grabbed my breasts and my butt in crowded streets. Some day, I will be drunk in public at night and I won't be scared.

I say this as I am drunk in a public place at night. But what's public and what's private for me anymore? My room is no more private than this terrace, with its thin walls and the door without a latch. Why else was I drinking whisky so silently? I haven't masturbrated since I got here. I can't even think about it anymore, I am so disinterested. I haven't even touched myself lovingly in a long time. I am not suited for public living. I need space.

It was close to ten when I left the terrace. I had missed dinner again. My stomach grumbled at the hope of leftover food as I walked to the mess hall to check if I could find something to eat. The cleaning ladies were there. I wobbled a bit, caught by surprise, and pretended like I was there for a drink of water, not food.

By the water cooler, I saw the women standing around the dining table full of empty bowls. They were scraping off the few grains of rice sticking to the bowls onto their tiffin box. Some were picking out half-eaten food from the dirty plates, wrapping it in newspaper, and putting it in their bags. Leftover green mush was certainly worse than green mush, which I thought was the absolute worst. How do they survive on it? It made me sad.

The cleaning woman who worked in my hostel was there; she waved at me. I asked her if she really went home so late every day. She nodded.

'It's not so bad, we get to take some food home this way,' she said. I smiled weakly.

I got back to the room hoping to ask Nita to give me a few Parle G biscuits that she is always munching on. She was not in her room though. Hope she ate dinner, wherever she is.

*

I washed clothes again today. It took me an hour and a half to wash fifteen pieces of clothing. My entire t-shirt was drenched in soapy water. I couldn't even toss the wet t-shirt in the laundry, I had nothing else to wear. I sat in a drenched tee later; my hands feel so weird that I can't hold a pen. How am I going to get any writing done if I spend so much time washing clothes?

I spoke to the hostel cleaning woman about washing my clothes for extra money. I agreed to give her double of what she charged for a bucket of clothes. The scene from the mess hall when she and the other cleaning staff scraped grains of rice from the empty bowls still haunted me. I wanted to help her in some way. Even though it was difficult to part with the cash, she certainly needed it more than I did. I don't have hungry children waiting for me at home.

Won't lie, it's a load lifted off my shoulders, too. I have realised that I won't be able to wash clothes twice a week and stay sane at the same time. Maybe it will help if I ease into it. I'm going to start by just washing my own underwear and maybe in the coming months I could build up to washing all of my clothes. Does it make sense for the protagonist in my novel to be this way too? She'd certainly be relatable if she felt this way, but nobody would take her seriously—all the talk about living with fewer means when she can't even wash clothes on her own? Maybe I could highlight it as a chore she doesn't enjoy and add a bit about how she missed the comfort of having a machine do her laundry.

11. Falling Sick

Week 4. I dreamt of Bhavya again. I dreamt that she called me, and I asked her why she broke up with me. I woke up feeling disgusted. I have the same dream every few months where I meet her or talk to her and ask her that same damn question every time: why did you end our relationship?

I never got to ask her this in real life. The only explanation I got from her was that she doesn't think of me anymore, an explanation my ego can't accept, especially when we talked intimately with each other just the day before the break up. And then there are other explanations that I know have caused the break up: Bhavya's mother's disapproval and the resulting shame and guilt; Bhavya's cowardice that paralysed her from standing up to her extended family and society to be herself; and Bhavya's desperate need to be normal so she could conform to the behaviours deemed appropriate by society. I understand these reasons but none of them, to my mind, is greater than our love. None of the reasons are big enough for us to quit on us.

And since I can't accept these reasons, my mind keeps looking for an explanation for the break up—a strong explanation for such a big crisis. I could call Bhavya right now and ask her to explain herself, but it won't help. She'll just tell me the reasons I already know and I don't believe—I don't even trust her anymore to believe any of it. I have to live with these imperfect reasons and somehow find a way to be satisfied. I guess it'll happen with time, the way my body calmed down with time.

In the aftermath of the breakup, in Ahmedabad, for a few months, my body reacted like the breakup didn't happen. When I'd see Bhavya's pic on my phone or read her message, or hear her recorded voice, I could feel my heart melt and I could feel a gush of warmth and love for her. I didn't know how to tell my body that she didn't appreciate that reaction anymore. She broke up with me on the phone so my last bodily memory of her was holding her tight; no wonder my body didn't understand what my mind knew. I spent every minute of the day aching for her, thinking about her, worrying if the world was treating her kindly.

I was desperate to find a way to explain to my body that she didn't want to be with me. I realised that I needed to do something physical that signalled to my body that I had to let her go. I thought about how people dealt with death and the cultural rituals that were performed during a funeral. I gave away her gifts to my friends, which didn't really make a difference because she was a bad gifter and I always hated her gifts. Then I really thought of the ending of the relationship as death and thought about performing Hindu rituals around death. My great idea, which feels silly now, was to buy flowers, say her name, and scatter them in the Sabarmati river; a practical modification of scattering ashes in the Ganga river. I did it, but it wasn't cathartic. The ache, the warmth, the love, the worry—they all remained.

I lost those feelings unexpectedly a few months later when I passed out drinking bootleg liquor. It was on the day of my would-be anniversary with Bhavya and I drank so much that I have no memory of eating, puking or going to sleep after that. I've never ever lost control drinking before, or had that much to drink. I don't know what happened, but the morning after when I woke up, I felt lighter and for the first time in a long time. I didn't think of Bhavya till much later in the day. Maybe it was because it was the first time I had really slept in years and shut down my brain completely. Or maybe passing out broke a thought pattern which helped rewire my brain. But the aching and the longing stopped that day.

So I know the dreams will stop someday too.

*

The seniors of the university are throwing a Fresher's party. Nita's been getting ready for the past two hours. Now her friends are here, giggling and clicking photos of each other. Nita and her friends look the same: they all have shaped eyebrows, waxed body hair, and straightened long hair. They are all wearing dresses, high heels, eyeliner and lipstick. Most women in the hostel today look like Nita, more or less.

I've felt the urge to dress that way too. Back in 12th standard, for a few years, I used to shave my body hair. I used to grow my hair long and tie it in a ponytail, and on occasions, I'd straighten it so it fell nicely on my shoulders. I have bushy eyebrows, and I used to shape them too. Most women I knew used to shape their eyebrows so it felt quite normal to do it. I even used to dress the way women around me dressed: I had a collection of long, three-quarter-sleeve kurtis and leggings. Since everyone around me dressed that way, and groomed themselves that way, it seemed like a mandatory part of growing into a woman.

But I noticed that the more I tried to look like the women around me, the more frustrated I got with my body. I have tiny eyes which look smaller when I wear eyeliner. My shoe size is UK 9; it was hard to find women's sandals in my size and my flat feet made it impossible to wear heels. I have broad shoulders that stick out in women's tops. It felt impossible to conform to the beauty standards that surrounded me and I constantly felt ugly.

Soon enough, I realised that I'd rather look beautiful to myself in a way that made my body feel comfortable and loved, than try to look pleasing to others. I cut my hair short, stopped shaping my eyebrows and shaving the hair on my arms and legs, and groomed myself in a way that made sense for me, my face, and my body. I found that I liked my fierce and bold eyebrows the way they were, and I liked the way the thin and uniform hair on my hand curved outwards slightly. I found that I loved wearing pants and jeans. I found that I liked wearing short kurtis with short sleeves, so now I have them stitched that way. My life changed the day I stopped looking for size 9 women's sandals and started wearing men's sneakers. The comfort!

I often get unsolicited advice from women about how I should groom myself. Some women ask me why I don't shape my eyebrows, some tell me outright that my eyebrows are ugly or make me look masculine. I laugh it off. I think it's easier to defy society's beauty standards as a queer woman with all my practice defying society's standards of compulsory heterosexuality and heteronormality. I have rebelled against society's notion about whom I should love; won't that give me the strength to rebel against society's notion about what I should look like?

I also think it's more possible as a queer woman to defy beauty standards because the idea of feminine beauty is so often depicted through a male gaze; beauty standards are a product of patriarchy meant for the gratification of heterosexual men. So what if those men don't find me attractive? Doesn't affect me one way or the other.

What did affect me is the notion that rejecting feminine beauty standards has made people perceive me as 'masculine', even though I can't be more comfortable in my female body, and I've never felt masculine. I think other queer women face this too, and that's how the stereotype of lesbians as dykes who are butch and masculine came to be. It's the perception of a society that has to compartmentalise everyone into 'his' or 'her' boxes. Does cutting my hair short and having body hair make me masculine? Those are just choices. I wish more women felt comfortable with the idea of beauty being plural. I wish they felt comfortable choosing not to shape their eyebrows if they didn't want to or to shape them a different way if they wished.

I heard Nita and her friends leave. I was invited to the fresher's party too, but I am not going. I'd rather be sad in my room than be sad at a party. A power outage again, probably a short circuit caused by the loud bass speakers from the party which were making the furniture vibrate. My head aches. There is no drinking water in the room, the only functioning water cooler is a five-minute walk away. I didn't want to venture out in the dark. I got drunk and thirsty waiting for the electricity, till I absolutely had to go out to get drinking water.

I didn't have a flashlight so I had to use the camera light in my phone. It was too focused on one spot; I couldn't see beyond a hundred centimetres. The whole place looked really eerie in the dark. I heard dogs bark from afar. A swarm of mosquitoes formed a halo over my head. Every time I looked into the pitch black darkness, I hallucinated that wild creatures would charge at me. So I swayed my hand around to make the flashlight move along my hands and throw light at everything for a second and again and again. I worried that moving the light around so much might make the stray dogs curious and want to chase me.

I reached the water cooler and quickly filled two bottles. I headed back, hugging the bottles and moving the camera light this way and that. People walking by stared at me; I made it look like the hand movement was part of my casual walking movement to avert their gaze. I returned to my room and lay in bed staring at the ceiling. I felt like a failure.

Things are easier in the morning when I can take the light for granted. I never had trouble with darkness before; why is it messing with me now? How did I go 24 years without ever feeling so helpless in the dark? Why am I scared of everything?

How would it work for my novel if the protagonist was scared of everything like I am? Comic relief? But these are such petty things. Why the hell am I scared of a grasshopper? There was a grasshopper in the toilet a couple of days ago and I walked to the other end of the hostel to use a different toilet each time that day. I think I am afraid of sudden movements, and all things that can move suddenly. An extension of my fear of confrontation, perhaps. I am scared that I am slow to react to movement and that makes me vulnerable to fast-moving insects and reptiles.

Power outages must definitely feature in my novel though. I am so dependent on power; every moment spent without it feels unproductive. Even if I am not directly using electricity to work, it's hard to work in the natural temperatures without the ceiling fan to cool me down. I am fortunate to have spent a few years without an air conditioner earlier. I have friends who can't survive summers without blazing their ACs. I was like that too when I lived with my parents. Living on my own though, I couldn't afford cold air, and I have gotten used to the heat now. The summer in Ahmedabad saw temperatures go up to 48 degrees celsius and I somehow survived without an AC by finding ways to cool myself naturally like washing my face every half an hour. I could have never imagined living in this hostel without an AC, if I weren't already living without one.

*

It's 3 am, and I can't sleep. It's so quiet, except for the sound of crickets, that I feel like I am the only one awake in the university.

Another power outage, but I can't care. My entire nasal cavity is blocked from a severe allergic reaction, probably from the violent washing of clothes. My body is going into self-preservation mode against every threat it perceives around me. I've been breathless for three nights straight. My mind is playing an annoying song in a loop, but the song is sped up and my mind is zooming in on the lyrics looking for new meanings. My body is restless, but I can't move or do anything that requires the burning of oxygen and become more breathless.

In the morning I have a high fever. So high that even Nita pitied me. She suggested I apply hot mustard oil on my feet to lower the fever and asked if she should help by heating the oil. I told her: I took a pill and I'll be fine. Is she crazy? No one who has ever truly lived alone can dream of applying oil on their feet. The lonely know their worst nightmare is falling and breaking a leg or a hip and becoming immobile. When you have no one to help you up from the bed or get food for you, you can't think of such things like applying oil on your feet. It's ridiculous.

After a bout of breathlessness came the stomach cramps. I've been vomiting all the food I am eating. I finally drove myself to the health centre in the university, but it was shut. It was two in the afternoon and they were probably out for lunch. I went there again in a few hours. The doctor scribbled some medicines while at least a hundred mosquitoes feasted on my blood. I would rather bear the stomach cramps next time than come to the health centre and get malaria.

Unicarbazan, I popped the pill from the strip. Side-effects include drowsiness and sleeplessness. Yesterday I fell asleep on my arm, was too drowsy to adjust myself. Today I am writing with a sore elbow, unable to fall asleep. Precaution: Don't mix with alcohol. Too late. I couldn't go too far with my allergies so I bought liquor from a shady local bar nearby. The seal of the bottle is broken—maybe it wasn't the best idea. But it won't be too bad to get used to country liquor, I might not be able to afford any better soon.

More stomach cramps and I really feel like dying.

*

A few days later, I still feel like dying, although I'm physically better. I don't know if I'm relieved that I'm not busy, that I won't feel guilty for wasting time being sad. Or I'm sad that I'm not busy and have a lot of time to stay sad. Maybe it would have helped to be a little busy, just enough to add variety to my feelings. It's like adding musical instruments to a symphony, always better when you can't single out one distinct sound. When I was young, I used to think that I could cry only when my body was filled with enough tears till it reached my eye-level. I would just stay sad imagining my legs filled up with tears, getting heavy. I could no longer get up and move, I spent most of my time on the bed with my heavy legs. In a few days, tears filled up my stomach, making me feel bloated.

Then a few days and I'd literally feel my heart drowning, it was quite real in the way it felt, and it got difficult to breathe. It got tricky then, I could feel my heart drown for weeks, even months, and every few days I'd be teased with a lump in my throat. Tears coming, almost teasing my eyes, and if I make crying faces, I'd probably tear up and cry for hours till the tears have drained out of my system. Or I could resist and let the tears drown me entirely, let the tears go to my brain and make me brain dead. Go into a coma for a few years, won't that be wonderful?

When I was in Ahmedabad, there were days I couldn't get out of bed. But the pressure to do something with my life was so overwhelming that I'd try to get into an accident just to get to stay in bed without bothering myself. I'd drive out on flyovers with my eyes closed, hoping to be hit by a car or a cow, or to drive off the flyover to at least injure myself seriously enough to give up on the year. But I couldn't keep my eyes closed for more than half a minute. Got too stressed out about the thought of the accident to really let it happen.

Won't it be great to feel some anxiety right now to balance this sinking, bloating, heaviness of being filled with tears? I need the lightness, the flying feeling from the fight or flight response when I think of my situation and how I've wasted my life. I can't afford to be sad. I don't have the time, money, and energy to be sad. If I stay sad, I'll fail the course and be unemployed, homeless, and lonely for the rest of my life. Now my blood is revolting, my heart is beating harsh against the tears like a drowning person gasping for air. I don't feel heavy anymore. I must pace around the room, worrying, sweating, giving myself a scare. It's the perfect harmony, to be able to drown and fly at the same time, like a dolphin. As long as I have depression and anxiety to balance each other out, I can thrive, even look graceful like a dolphin.

*

I dreamed of lizards last night. A dozen lizards crawled inside the plastic mesh layer of my sanitary pad. When I squatted to pee, I saw them wagging their tongues at me, their tongues covered in my blood. I pulled the pad and tried to drown the lizards in tap water. But the water made them grow in size till they broke out of my pad and spat fireballs of my blood like dragons. The dragons started laughing and they sounded exactly like Saisree and her roommates who teased each other and laughed in their room from six in the morning (on a Sunday). They were laughing when I woke up at eleven. I ran my finger through my vagina and smelled for blood. There was no blood (and probably no lizards)

I squat for real, I try to catch the dead leaves that fall through the toilet window, thinking of the time Saisree kept neem leaves in the bathroom to wrap her sanitary pad. Or was it to clean herself? My knees hurt. I go through the day feeling incomplete. Something is different. I went to sleep again and woke up in a panic, my neighbour's loud laughing was drowned by a wailing that assaulted my eardrums. Did I still live in the hostel of a public university? Why do I hear the screaming lungs of a baby?

It's probably a dream.

I fell back asleep and imagined a baby in my room. She poked my eye so I poked hers which made her cry even louder than before. The baby spoke, she said, 'Go look Saisree in the eye. Tell her to shut up. Tell her you'll fling me so high, I'll be out of sight.' Then the baby went flying into space, out of sight, like I flung her. As she flew she said, 'Nobody suspects babies of having an inner voice.'

I heard a baby laugh when I woke up, it was four in the evening. I knocked on Saisree's door, still drowsy from having had 10 hours of interrupted sleep. She opened the door with a baby in her arms.

'Are babies allowed in the hostel?' I asked her. It was a very stupid question to ask, who really cared about what was allowed.

'We brought her from the village because she is sick,' Saisree said. 'We are taking her to the doctor tomorrow morning and from there she'll go straight to the village.'

'The baby is making a lot of noise,' I said. What a stupid thing to say, again. It's a baby…

'Sorry…' she said.

To escape the baby, I ventured out of the campus, to get a haircut. I usually get my haircut in the cheapest expensive salon, but I can't afford that. I drove around searching for smaller beauty parlours that usually operated out of the parlour lady's house. The first one told me she doesn't cut short hair, which was weird. I asked why. She said she doesn't know how to. The next three beauty parlours said the same thing. I tried approaching a men's salon, and they told me they won't cut a woman's hair. I returned feeling defeated.

I really needed the haircut. My sinuses have flared up from all the sweat that soaks my thick hair. I should save up some money to buy a blow dryer to blow dry the sweat off my hair. Or I could just shave my head. Only if my hands had the fine-motor skills to handle a razor, or I'd cut my ear off like Van Gogh. Won't hear this baby scream at the top of its lungs if I cut my ear off, and it would be less of a bother than the sinus. I bet Van Gogh had similar options and those who call him insane just don't know his situation.

My back is killing me again. My breasts are in pain too. Maybe it's PMS, though I really think it is this cheap bra. When I needed a bra, my mother took me to a hawker who sold lingerie in the open Andheri street market. My size is 40D but I only own bras that are of size 38B because hawkers can only fit sizes 32, 34, 36, and 38 in the limited space they have on their cart.

When I point out to my mother that she can afford to buy me a bra that fits, it triggers her anxiety. She has me do mental maths of all the savings she needs to do if she has to survive on it after retirement. Her maths is fundamentally flawed: she assumes all the costs will inflate but the value of her assets won't. It's not worth pointing out though because her rant is really not about retirement, it's just her anxiety. After all the mental maths, she'd say, 'It's not like I can expect my children to take care of me when I'm old. I'll probably have to take care of you and your brother,' alluding to our disability, perhaps. Can't argue with her though; so far she's been right, we haven't amounted to much.

*

The rest of the evening was spent listening to the baby cry while Saisree and her roommates laughed. I thought about the last time I was near a baby, probably when my brother was a baby. I wondered what this baby will grow into. Probably a version of Saisree and her roommates, growing up with the same people around her all her life. I wonder how different it would be if the baby were a boy. The parents of the baby would have probably travelled to the city to see a doctor themselves if she was a boy instead of sending her through Saisree and keeping her in the filthy hostel. Or not. I think these stereotypes don't capture the nuances of reality. In reality, everyone behaves in their own different way with different genders.

My parents told me they wanted a girl when I was born. I thought it was progressive of them when I was young, but now I know what they really meant when they said they wanted a girl. My father wanted a secretary-maid who he could dominate, who typed out what he dictated and served him food. My mother wanted a doll she could dress up. When my mother was young, she wanted to dress differently and have different hairstyles, but my grandmother didn't let her. She wanted to live that through me.

While I was her doll, she never bought me one. All my friends had dolls and I wanted one just to fit in. She said she won't buy me a doll because she didn't want me to be overly emotional and sensitive like other girls. And somehow not owning dolls would make me tough. Not owning dolls was the first time I didn't fit in with others. It was the beginning of my life as an outsider.

My family tried to mould my gender expression in confusing ways. My grandmother set out to make me more feminine and my mother, tangled in misogyny, wanted to make me more masculine.

My grandmother always conjured my future-mother-in-law to get me to be feminine. She'd say:

my future-mother-in-law won't like it if I didn't wear jewellery, or my future-mother-in-law won't like it if I had short hair so I had to grow my hair long. My future-mother-in-law would hate the way I sat, I needed to put my feet down and stick my knees close together like I was guarding my best kept secret between my legs. I don't know if I hate jewellery and long hair because they were forced on me or if they needed to be forced on me because I hated them. But I just hate them on myself, even though I think jewellery and long hair suited many men and women. I loved the way my grandmother's diamond-studded earrings and nose ring suited her; she kept them very clean and sparkly.

My mother shamed me for being girly every time I cried. According to her, expressing emotions was a feminine weakness. But my mother cried every night when my drunk father said mean things to her. I asked her why she was allowed to cry, and she said she was crying from anger and rage-crying wasn't feminine. All through my childhood till a few years ago, I've only cried when I was hurt physically after a family member pinched me or whacked me. I started crying from emotional hurt only after I opened up emotionally following my relationship with Bhavya. Till then, I also believed crying was a feminine weakness. I think being able to express emotions is a strength now. Glad I grew out of my mother's misogyny.

In my childhood, my mother taught me how to ride a cycle. She cycled to school in her village when she was young and she wanted the same for me. At 14, as a young student in Delhi, I also started riding the cycle to school and tuition classes. I preferred cycling because the alternative was going to school in the school bus and my brand of dyslexia made it hard for me to find the right bus that went to my house from among the fleet of buses parked outside the school. I had to either memorise the bus number or remember the bus driver's face—both were impossible and I wasn't smart enough to find coping mechanisms just yet.

None of my classmates cycled to school or to tuition, not even the boys. Probably because Delhi was a lot more dangerous than my mother's village. So many strange men have stalked me while I was riding to school. One approached me and asked to come to a quieter lane with him, and I almost had to fight him off. When I told my mother, she said, 'That's how men are, just ignore them.'

When I was 17, I commuted alone in Bombay's local trains. One night when I was walking from the train station to my house, a stranger grabbed my butt several times. He followed me to my building and stood next to me as I waited for the lift. I knew he would assault me if I entered the lift with him. I ran back to the busy street and kept running for half an hour. When I came back, he was not there.

I was too scared to commute alone after that. I needed my mother to help me. Maybe there was a different, safer way to commute. I talked to her about the rape statistics in India and I compared it to the west to emphasise how underreported rape was in India and how unsafe it was for women in Delhi and Bombay. She said, 'Rape doesn't happen in the west because women have loose morals and willingly have sex with strangers. They just call it rape when they don't like it.'

'If I don't want to be raped, I should just be more willing to have sex with strangers, then?'

'No, that's against Indian culture.'

I couldn't get through to her. In hindsight, I wonder why I thought she'd understand my sexuality when she couldn't even understand the concept of sex and consent. I was stupid.

I'm starting to like the baby. Hope she has a nice childhood, although I'm sceptical. Half the parents just have kids because society wants them to, it's no wonder they are not wonderful parents. My parents thought keeping me alive was good parenting. But before I say they were bad parents, I think about the horrible daughter that I am. I always wonder if they regretted having me, that if they knew how I'd turn out they probably won't want me. I'm worse than the worst nightmare they had for me. They wanted me to study science and have babies. I wanted them to understand and accept who I am. Maybe we are even?

12. Studying

Month 2. Midterms here, already. I have done nothing all week but stay locked inside the room. I plan to study in the morning and do something else in the evenings. But I don't get any studying done in the morning, and stay shut inside the room in the evenings to compensate; I end the days accomplishing nothing and feeling worthless.

I have a test tomorrow and I have to read five research papers to write it. I can't read past the first page of any of the papers. Dull academic writing just doesn't appeal to me. For me, to apply the enormous effort of reading, the material has to be engaging. How do I convince myself that it is going to be worth it? I tried explaining to myself that I'll flunk out if I don't read, but that only made me nervous.

I updated my resumé yesterday and spent the evening looking for jobs. I have a few months of experience in auditing balance sheets and a few months in web design and cinema theatre management. These jobs have a flood of applicants; nothing that sets me apart from them. The pay is terrible, the work is dull. I need another skill. Today I thought maybe I can learn data analytics online till this semester ends, but after searching for courses I remembered how I mixed up numbers during an auditing articleship. Data analytics might not be a good choice for me. I went back to studying for the midterms.

I don't have impostor syndrome; I am an impostor. I don't belong here. I can't read. I can't memorise. I can't write. But, I'm an impostor anywhere. I was an impostor studying accounting, I wasn't suited for that at all. I was an impostor in school, an impostor everywhere I worked. Am I less of an impostor here than in all those other places? I have enjoyed all the lectures so far, and I'm engaging really well with the curriculum. I'll just do badly at the exams, that's all. I'm learning. I know things. It's not that bad.

Wish I had a better, more positive relationship with reading. But my complicated relationship with reading started with a complicated relationship with books. Nobody in my house read books when I was a child. My father would occasionally read Tamil magazines, and my grandparents read the newspaper—and that's all the reading I've seen in my house. We owned zero books. When I was young, I was obsessed with stories. I refused to sleep till my grandfather told me a story from his youth in his village. When he ran out of stories, I started reading Indian comic books. I'd spend all my pocket money buying issues of *Tinkle.*

When I grew out of those stories, around 8, I was ready for my first novel. I bought it at a second-hand book sale in my building complex in Chennai: *Invisible Man* by H G Wells. It took me 45 minutes to read a page and three years to read that novel. At that time, the girls in my building complex were reading the Harry Potter books which I wanted to read too but I couldn't get past the first chapter. I was too dyslexic for the unfamiliar words that were part of the magical Harry Potter universe. This was before the movies came out, so when one of the girls called me Neville Longbottom, I had no idea it was meant as an insult. I eventually finished the series, but reading and holding on to that much information to understand the story was not worth it.

After *Invisible Man* and the Harry Potter series, even though reading was torture, I felt a peculiar attraction to books that made me want to read more. I was 13 at the time, living in Delhi. My mother didn't want to spend a lot on books so she took me on an hour-long car ride from our house in Vasant Kunj to the Red Fort area where she'd heard there was a second-hand book sale every Sunday. It was a crowded road and we couldn't find parking so we parked far away and walked to the area where there were books laid out on the road like vegetables in street markets. My mother and I were the only women there.

I bent down to look at books when a man who passed by caressed my butt. Then the next man who passed caressed my butt. Every single man who passed by caressed my butt and my mother's. I told her I was uncomfortable with people touching me and saw that she had not even noticed it till then. She asked me to ignore it and to select the books I wanted to buy quickly. I didn't even have time to read the blurbs. I had a few minutes to select the books by their covers and go. I picked six books, and my mother let me buy four.

In the car, I said it was strange the way the men were touching us.

'Men are like that,' she said. 'You'll get used to it.'

'Why should I get used to something I don't like?'

'It's just like that in this world,' she said. 'I stayed with a family as a paying guest when I got a job at a bank after my graduation. The man in the house used to squeeze my breasts at night. I would just lie there pretending to sleep and let him do it. What's the point of saying anything?'

'You could have left the house, right?'

'No, it was a nice house otherwise, everyone was so nice to me.'

I never asked to buy books again. I waited till I was 16 and was able to travel on my own to a bookstore where I got enough time to browse and buy books. I never read the four books I bought that day. I tried, but I didn't like them.

I was 16 when I discovered books that I liked. It started with a trip to the Landmark bookstore in Infiniti mall near my house in Bombay. The store had a big poster of the cover of *Clockwork Orange* by Anthony Burgess and I was so drawn to it that I bought the book. Reading *Clockwork Orange* also started me off on watching classic films starting with Stanley Kubrick's adaptation of the book. In the next few years, I read obsessively; enamoured by Russian Realism at first, I read many works by Tolstoy, Chekov, Gogol and Dostoyevsky. Then I read 20th-century European writings by Kafka, Sartre and Camus while I enjoyed the French New Wave cinema of Truffaut, Varda and Godard. I remember feeling exhilarated every day those few years, blown away by the books and cinema I was immersing myself in, thrilled to interact with works that gave me a language to understand despair.

Now every time I get a rejection letter from a publishing house or a literary magazine, I tell myself that I am still catching up with the literature universe. I still had a lot to explore, experiment, learn, and experience about storytelling because I started reading so late and I read so slowly. I started writing when I was 14, so I've been writing longer than I've been reading, which is weird.

*

First midterm test is tomorrow. The pressure to study was so unbearable that I couldn't stay in the room. I've been loitering outside all day. Now I feel like a parent who returns home to find that their kid hasn't done any class homework. I'm mad at myself.

For most exams of my life, I've started studying only at 2 am, the morning of the exam. In the days leading up to the exam, I'm so nervous I'm going to fail that I binge eat, play freecell on my phone, watch movies, or loiter outside talking nonsense. It feels like I'm trying to escape the self-loathing monster I become while trying to study. At 2 am, the morning of the exam, after heavy doses of caffeine and nicotine, I feel my nerves pulsing through my body, and I become this monster who can suddenly skim through a hundred pages of text to jot down as many points as I am likely to remember. Then I sleep from six to eight and before the exam, I revise the points I've written down. I've been doing this consistently and helplessly for every exam in my life so far, and I've written every exam sleep-deprived without exception. Although it could be argued that I'm sleep deprived on most days. But it's bad during exams; I've needed to wash my face to stop myself from falling off the chair into deep slumber.

It's 10 pm now and I'm brewing coffee. It's going to be a long night.

*

My midterms went okay. I found summaries of most research papers online. Those summaries coupled with my extensive lecture notes were enough to write answers somehow. The university professors offered to give me accommodations for my learning disabilities, but I turned them down. It didn't feel right. There are so many students in my class who did their schooling and Bachelor's programme in their native languages, and they are here at the university studying in a Master's programme where the medium of instruction is English. It's hard for them to write in English, but they don't get any accommodations. How are their issues any different than mine? It's the same decoding and encoding in different languages. They also can't read as fast as others or have the extensive vocabulary of European academics. I can't accept accommodations till they get accommodations too. I wonder how they are coping with coursework; I should tell them about my trick of getting paper summaries online.

*

A girl keeps ogling me. I always find her at the mess hall, regardless of how early or late I go there. She sits by her food and just stares at it, as if staring would make it any more appetising. She shakes her leg nervously, and without moving her head, she peeks in my direction every few minutes. When I look at her, she widens her eyes, as if I've caught her doing something wrong, and she lowers her head quickly to look at the food again. When I leave the table, she rushes to the communal sink to wash her plate next to me every single day.

I think she has a crush on me.

Today we were standing in the queue to get the plates when I see her leave her place in the queue so she could stand behind me. I could feel her heavy breath on the back of my neck, which made my hair flutter slightly. I feel nervous, like I am about to be touched. She grazed my back gently with her elbow every few minutes as she pretended to look for something in her backpack. I froze, unsure what to do.

I think she is too shy to talk to me so she's signalling to me to initiate a conversation. I'm very lonely and I don't know any women interested in women in the city, but there is something about the way she looks at me that upsets me. It's not a gaze filled with curiosity or emotional eagerness. It feels like lust. Like she wants me to satisfy her carnally. Nothing wrong with that, it's just not for me.

Lust confuses and alienates me. I've never felt it, yet it is the first thing people assume about me when I talk about my sexuality. I know this because when I came out to friends who were men, they always sent me pictures of women in tight yoga pants that outlined the shape of their backsides like I'd enjoy the pictures. Or they winked at me when an attractive girl passed by, and I never understood what the wink was about and they had to point at the girl for me to put it together. It makes me feel uncomfortable, and I don't know how to explain myself.

I understand where they're coming from. When I talk about my sexuality, it probably looks like sex is a big part of my life or an important part at least. But I barely ever think about sex, and I don't look at women sexually. I definitely think about hiding my sexuality more than I think about sex.

I know nothing is wrong with me, and I know I have a healthy relationship with sex. If sex were a car ride, for a lot of people it would be like their daily commute to work or their weekend grocery run, a necessary routine. For some, it is like using an app like Uber to order the kind of ride they want, with room for a lot of exploration and adventure. For me, however, sex is like going on a road trip with someone you trust. It is a physical journey and a journey within. It is a journey you undertake to bond with someone and know them better. It is a spiritual journey that lets me escape everyday life; when it happens, I feel teleported to a space where time doesn't exist and there is an endless amount of skin to touch.

I sometimes felt lonely within the queer circles I was part of in Bombay and Ahmedabad which were mostly dominated by men and their discussions focused on their sexual encounters. I also feel lonely in queer circles when they talk about marriage rights like that would be the government's supreme gesture to restore equality between heterosexuals and homosexuals. I expected the queer community to challenge society's notion of what a relationship was, in the way they have challenged society's notion of sex and sexuality. I was really hoping for the queer community to experiment with different configurations of relationships and family. Like being in a relationship with someone and raising children with someone else, or living with your friends or your parents while being in a relationship with someone—these could be legitimate long-term reconfigurations of relationships and family that's outside the heteronormal marriage.

I should write a novel or a short story about a futuristic world with family configurations outside the heteronormal marriage.

*

I was in my room earlier today when the door fell open. Saisree wanted me to help her friend with her MPhil thesis. I followed them to their room. They were making banana chips, I had some. Delicious.

Saisree wanted me to help her use a word processor to find and replace words in her friend's thesis. Find the name of an African-sounding hospital. Replace it with the name of a hospital in Hyderabad. Apparently, the thesis was originally written by someone in Nigeria. Her brother had sourced it for her from somewhere. I asked her if her professor won't catch her for plagiarism. She didn't understand what plagiarism was. But I'm guessing this dissertation was never published in Nigeria so anyone could use it as their own. Didn't know there was a market for unpublished dissertations. I have to write one in my fourth semester, maybe I can sell it?

I'm continuously surprised by how enterprising Saisree and her friends are. I don't blame them for cheating because they did their schooling in their native language, and it's not easy to switch to English as the medium of instruction in the university. How can they be expected to write a thesis in English? And the professors can't teach something as basic as how to write. It's nice that Saisree's friend found a loophole, but how useful is it going to be? Even if she uses her MPhil to get a job, what if the job involves writing? What will she do then?

*

I went out for coffee and samosa and saw protesters chanting 'Rohith Vermula is Alive'. I feel awful about what happened to Rohith a few months ago that led him to take his own life. I won't pretend to understand the caste complexities of the issue, but I can imagine how lonely he must have felt, helplessly fighting against the oppressive system.

I'd protest with them if there weren't enough students protesting because I believe what happened shouldn't be ignored. But I also don't want to join in because I don't think sacking authorities and institutionalising a committee that protects minorities will solve the problem. It won't stop political parties from indoctrinating students with their caste and communal politics. I think it'd be better to have the student union cut all ties from local and national politics. That way at least we won't be fighting age-old battles. My brother said that's how student union elections worked in his college in Delhi.

Deep down, for someone who concerns herself with social justice, I'm embarrassed how little I know about caste. I've been meaning to educate myself, but I just haven't found the time for it. I'm uncomfortable that I'd get caught protesting about something that I don't know anything about. Is being outraged by the events that led to Vermula's suicide enough to protest it? I don't know, I really have no context about caste discrimination in educational institutions. I should really stop taking myself seriously when I don't know of suffering outside of my own loneliness.

Or I don't know, maybe I don't feel like protesting in general. To protest, one must hope for change—I can't anymore. I haven't even been to an LGBT+ rights protest in the last two years. Maybe I don't have the passion in me to protest anymore. I can't take a stand on these weak shaky legs. I can't pretend to care about the outside world when my own life is in crisis. I'm emotionally exhausted.

I also don't have much hope for universities being safe spaces for anyone from a minority community. My professors are great and have such progressive views about human rights—but it's all talk. They can effect change, form a committee that takes disciplinary action against any student or faculty member who is harassing or bullying those from minority communities. But they haven't, I don't know why. My own professors definitely have the authority to create a safe space within our department. The least they can do is tell students they won't tolerate harassment and bullying, that they'll help women, lower-caste, disabled, and LGBT+ students fight institutional oppression. They talk about human rights much like my school teachers taught me about caste. Like it has nothing to do with our lives.

*

I used to call Bhavya my soulmate, like one would when they were in love with someone. She used to call me her soulmate too, but that probably changed for her through the course of the relationship. When she broke up with me on a phone call, it was so dispassionate, I realised that I couldn't have meant much to her. A phone-call break up of a three-year relationship only made sense to me in the context of the relationship being superficial or transactional like sex work or an extramarital affair—and maybe that's how it was for her in the end. When she kept meeting me in secret while knowing that everyone in her life would disapprove of it, it must have felt a lot like an extramarital affair or a visit to a prostitute—to her it probably felt like a dishonourable digression from 'real life'.

But I maintained that she was my soulmate till the end. And I used to feel overwhelmed and elated every time I thought I had a soulmate, even though Bhavya was fickle about our relationship and totally neglected me in the last year. I definitely noticed her neglect when she didn't even call to check how I was when I was hospitalised for two weeks and the doctors suspected I had Swine Flu. I should have ended the relationship then because it was clear she didn't care how I was, but because I believed she was my soulmate, I thought it was a tiny bump in my lifelong relationship with my soulmate. I realise now that my way of thinking then was very close to the logic domestic abuse victims use to continue living with their partners.

Now I wonder if my love for Bhavya was anything more special than just two young people falling in love. I made it feel more special by calling her my soulmate and therefore placing our relationship in the larger-than-life narrative of Romeo and Juliet, or Leo and Sophia Tolstoy, and a host of other soulmate relationships that have inspired awe in me. It felt like our relationship was a continuation of those. I now wonder if I was in love with Bhavya or with the narrative of being someone's soulmate. What could be better than feeling like a part of something larger than life to inflate one's sense of ego?

But the narrative came at a cost. I was making the relationship out to be something it wasn't: I was putting a lot of pressure on it and evaluating everything that happened as a bump in the 'larger scheme of things' when there were clear signs that there may not be a 'larger scheme of things' between Bhavya and me. If I'm ever in another relationship, it's going to be about the here and the now with the past as context. I won't live in the future.

Soulmate wasn't the only larger-than-life narrative that had me under its spell, patriotism was another one. I used to feel an overwhelming patriotic pride about being Indian, but what is India if not a wonky line on a map? Why did I feel proud about what India represents when a lot of the history happened before I was born but somehow it feels like a personal achievement. Why does being an Indian citizen feel like such a big part of me when I can easily sign a few papers, book a flight ticket, and stop being an Indian citizen? Now I realise that I didn't want my life to end with me; I wanted my life to be part of the history of this nation because that way my ego could span centuries and accommodate a portion of the world and I could feel immense rather than my small suffering self.

Living in Bombay felt like that too. The city feels overwhelming. Because important things happened in the city, I felt important just being in the city when I was doing absolutely nothing important. I find that a lot of my friends who live in Bombay can't get over the fact of living in that city. The feeling is so powerful, it feels worthy of the ridiculous rent. But I managed to snap out of the spell. Although some vestiges of the spell remain. Now when I live in Hyderabad and when I used to live in Ahmedabad, at times I felt second-rate like I didn't matter so much. I would miss the larger-than-life narrative of Bombay—a city that made me feel miserable, but important.

But I'm growing out of it. No more soulmate, nation, lineage, caste, community, politics—nothing larger than life to inflate my sense of self. I don't feel swell, but I feel calm. Not being part of a narrative gives me the freedom to be myself without constantly trying to fit myself into the narrative. I find that others can be part of such narratives and still keep their sense of self in check, but I go overboard.

It feels silly now but there was a time when I used to deny the effects of climate change. I used to think climate change wasn't a big deal; even if snow caps melted, the world would just morph into a different world, like it has many times now, so it wasn't a big deal. I was 14 at the time, and I wanted to be rich to rid my life of my parents' influence. Climate change challenged the capitalist success narrative that I saw myself in, and I didn't like it. No logic was going to make me believe in climate change when I was sold out on the promises of the material world.

I know now the rate at which the climate is changing can have catastrophic results. It's embarrassing to me that I ever denied it, that I refused to consider scientific facts and evidence. But denying climate change has given me an insight into feelings like xenophobia and homophobia. Xenophobia is a response to nationalism getting challenged like homophobia is a response to family values getting challenged. Tell a homophobic person that homosexuality is seen in many animal species and they'd still call it unnatural, like I refused to see facts about climate change. How do two men or women raising a child together challenge anyone's family values? But the nature of these narratives is so absolute and specific that they'd be threatened by such a modification.

It's great to be part of something larger than life, but these narratives need to be plural, accommodating, and abstract. We need multiple meanings of what it means to be a good person, of what it means to be kind, of what it means to be beautiful. If we can broaden our idea of nationalism and family values, we can all feel secure in our identities without feeling threatened by others.

I should write a story about this. Just imagining a world of plural narratives for different ideologies would be a great mental exercise!

13. Dating

Month 3. I haven't felt like writing these days, or doing anything, really. I try to go about my day, attend lectures, study—all without breaking down. I'm not always successful, but I'm still here. As I write this, while feeling everything I'm feeling, I can't help but think that I'm overreacting. I keep asking myself: Is my life really as bad as I think it is?

As a woman who isn't afraid to show her emotions, I've been told I'm overreacting so often that it has become a voice in my head. I've been told that I have to put my sorrow in context of those more unfortunate. Like everything I feel is okay and can be ignored because there are other people who have it worse than me. The truth is, I don't know how those people's inner lives are, how easily they bounce back in face of adversity, and whether they are suffering at all. All I know is my sorrow. My sorrow of never ever experiencing a minute of peace. My sorrow of never finding a place to rest, live, and prosper without worrying about eviction. My sorrow of never being seen, never being loved, and never reaching my potential. My sorrow of isolation. My sorrow of being broken inside, hollow, never believing in hope. This sorrow is worthy. My depression is real.

It is mid-September, and it has rained most days all month. I haven't seen the sun in two weeks. I wouldn't be writing today if something absolutely bizarre hadn't happened to me just now. All month with heavy rains, the toilets and bathrooms have been infested with all sorts of creatures, but mainly, lizards and grasshoppers. I find it difficult to pee or bathe with beady reptile and insect eyes staring at me. So when there is a lizard or a grasshopper in thc toilct in my wing, I go to a toilet in a different wing to pee. This whole process takes 20 minutes every time.

All the toilets in my floor had bugs this morning, so I went to the ground floor. I waited outside an occupied toilet for a few minutes. A girl walked out and I went in. I saw a huge frog in the drain hole of the Indian commode. I called the girl and said, 'Excuse me! Can you also see a frog here?'

She came back, looked at it, made a disgusted face and said, 'God! Did I just pee on a frog?'

'I guess so,' I said, leaving. Don't want the frog, dripping pee, jumping on me.

I don't mean to judge the poor girl but how absent-minded do you have to be to pee on a frog? Or am I hyper-aware, needlessly noticing every detail of my surroundings? When I first came to the hostel, I noticed that there was a bird's nest on the WiFi device in the hallway. It had been there long enough for all the bird eggs to have hatched. When I pointed it out, most people were shocked; nobody had noticed the nest, or the slow WiFi speed. Not the students, not the hostel staff.

Last week, when I noticed the toilet lights flickering, I saw a dead lizard hanging on the open wire of the tubelight and getting electrocuted every few minutes making the light flicker. There was a buzzing sound as the dead lizard would tremble convulsively against the flickering light… it was horrifying! And nobody saw it. Nobody notices anything. They just trust that everything is fine and they go about their lives. I feel like every little insect is out to get me so I have my eyes peeled looking for threats in my surroundings. Is it my anxiety that makes me want to notice everything around me and prepare for all that could go wrong. Or is it my 'Brahmin' X-ray vision? Looking for hygiene violations the way I was taught to by my family. Or have I just never trusted my surroundings to keep me safe? I live like I'm in the jungle. I sleep like I'm in the jungle, with one eye open.

*

It is 2 am; I can't go to sleep. My back aches. The power went off two hours ago. I'm lying in a pool of my sweat. If the power doesn't come back soon, my sinuses will act up again.

With or without power, I haven't been able to sleep easily ever since I got here. Is my insomnia back? I really hope not. Last time I had insomnia for six months and it absolutely wrecked my sense of wellbeing. It was the time when I had dropped out of accountancy and failed out of a Master's programme in Economics. Bhavya's mother had just found out about us, and that had ended our relationship. I stayed up night after night compulsively writing letters to Bhavya's mother in my head, explaining my intentions with Bhavya, professing my love for her in ways that feel silly now. I asked Bhavya if I should write that letter to her mother. She laughed it away, and I pretended that it was a joke too.

Then I stayed up having conversations in my head with Bhavya's best friend Yukti. She didn't like me, but Bhavya's mother liked her. Yukti was a literature graduate, and I asked her to edit the manuscript of my first novel just to meet her. I wanted to ask Yukti to talk to Bhavya's mother about me and explain that homosexuality was not a disorder, and that I meant well for her daughter. But reading my manuscript made her dislike me more, and reading her editorial feedback made me dislike her. I later found out that it was Yukti who'd told Bhavya's mother about my relationship with Bhavya in the initial months of our relationship. She just let Bhavya's mother's hate and homophobia brew and bubble till it lashed out against us. I don't know why Yukti did that, but Bhavya still wanted to be friends with her. I still don't know what I make of all this, but it makes me very angry.

So I stayed up, paranoid, looking for jobs and career paths that'd give me the opportunity to migrate with Bhavya to another country where I could marry her, like that would solve all our issues. All I wanted to do was elope with her like in the movies where parents are against a couple's union. But to marry her legally, we'd both have to find jobs and migrate to some western country and spend decades there till we became citizens of that country. It takes the cinematic and romantic edge off eloping.

I knew I was losing Bhavya, and realised staying up all night wouldn't fix anything. I decided to go with the flow, and let the situation resolve itself. In hindsight, it feels silly that I was losing sleep over a situation I had no control over.

I miserably watched as Bhavya and I drifted apart over the next year. I regret not ending the relationship myself, but I'm glad I didn't end it too. If I had ended things with Bhavya, I'd always feel guilty about abandoning her. Because she ended things, I can feel anger instead.

*

I've found that Indian dating apps are the worst way to find lesbian or bisexual women. But that's not stopping me from downloading them again today.

Most of the dating apps now have an option to connect with people of the same sex, even though there are barely any women looking for women on it. From my interactions with women on these apps, I know how most conversations will play out. Either a woman would start by saying sexually provocative things right away which mostly means that the woman is actually a man catfishing and getting off. Or a woman would tell me that they are bicurious which means they changed their settings to match with the same sex after a bad experience with the opposite sex. They'd try to force intimacy with me which feels as cringey and painful as it sounds. Usually, the conversation dies within a day and their settings switch back to the default.

I went on a date with a 'bicurious' woman once who was very keen to meet me. Even before we could order coffee, she said, 'I'm not attracted to you.'

'Yeah, that's okay, me too. I only find attraction once I get to know someone,' I said, like I was an expert in the subject of attraction.

'Oh, so it can happen later?' She said, 'I was worried.'

'Why worried?'

'I've dated men,' she said, 'but I don't know if I found them attractive so I thought I should experiment with women. Just to be clear, I have no attraction for you.'

'Ok, should I leave or do you want to order coffee?'

'No, stay!' She said, 'I'm just saying that maybe like you said, I'll know if I'm attracted to you if we experimented.'

'Okay?'

Awkward silence.

'So, then, what are we?'

'I don't know,' I said. 'Friends?'

'Are we going to experiment?'

'Sorry, I'm not comfortable with that,' I said.

We had coffee in an awkward silence and then we shared a cab in an awkward silence. She got out on a turning and said she'd walk home; it made me feel like I'd stalk her if I found out where she lived. Before leaving, she asked, 'Are we together? What should I tell my friends?'

'Let's meet again and see how it goes,' I said and blocked her number.

Just thinking of the encounter makes me cringe. Such a weird human being completely obsessed with what she is supposed to feel, what she is supposed to do, and what she is supposed to call our relationship.

She basically wanted to treat me like a piece of litmus paper to see which colour she'd turn while taking no responsibility for my feelings. I'm not emotionally strong enough to be someone's experiment.

After I met her, I swore off women and changed my settings to match with men. She got in my head, and I wondered how I was sure I wasn't attracted to men when I'd never been with one. So I started talking to men, and I even went on a date with one in Ahmedabad. He met me near my house and I drove us to old Ahmedabad. We had tea at Lucky restaurant which is this weird place that has graves of 100-year-old dead bodies between tables and a painting by M F Hussain on the wall. My date told me M F Hussain used to have tea at the restaurant often and gifted them that painting. When I told him I write fiction, he made me read his godawful poetry on his laptop that reeked of teenage angst: every poem was about a battle which, guessing from what I knew about him, was a lazy metaphor for an exam or a girl.

At the end of the date, he leaned in to kiss me, and I panicked. I had the urge to run away as fast as I could, as far as I could. I told him I wasn't comfortable, made an excuse, and rushed home where I cried and cried like I'd been betrayed, like I was in danger. It was an overreaction, but that's how I felt at the thought of kissing a man. Even though the date with the man was much better than the date with the woman, when she asked me if we could experiment, I didn't feel as uncomfortable.

I don't know what this means for me, but I guess it means I should stay off dating apps. But I'm starved for attention and intimacy. I just want to flirt with someone and feel like there is even a minute possibility that I can have a relationship with someone again. I just want to feel like there are options for me, that there is a remote possibility that I could fall in love again. That there are people out there who might find me charming and worthy.

The world conspires to bring straight couples together. Friends set each other up, dating apps gamify their union, old aunties gossip about possible matches, and their parents find suitable bachelors for them. The possibility of finding someone must feel so palpable to heterosexuals in this heteronormative world. On the other hand, the world conspires to keep gay couples apart. We have friends telling on us, dating apps disappointing us, aunties shaming us, and our parents forbidding us from seeing someone even if they suit us.

I want to find love, but where do I look? Gay men have Grindr which has its own flaws but it's still something. The only place I've seen lesbians is at Pride, and it is so messed up to go to a pride march to try to meet someone. It's creepy.

There is no hope for me.

*

Saisree keeps barging into my room without knocking, startling my poor heart. Sometimes it's to borrow a pen. Sometimes she asks me to get rice and vegetables for her and her friends from the mess. Other times it's to get me to proofread her assignment. Today she came into my room to ask me to run for the mess secretary position of the South mess.

'But, I don't want to be a mess secretary.'

'No, you won't be,' she said. 'This is just to have enough candidates to show we had a fair election.'

'Can't your friends run for the position?'

'You have to be a student in the university to run,' she said. 'And it looks better if it's not all local Telugu girls.'

I went with her to the warden's room to fill out my application. There were five nominees in total and the warden would pick the candidate by the end of the week.

'What if she picks me?' I asked Saisree.

'She won't... we have setting.'

The warden called me back to tell me I was disqualified from applying for the mess secretaryship because I hadn't paid my mess dues since I'd joined the university. Apparently, my name was also on the notice board, and now I have to pay a fine along with the mess fees for three months. I owed them close to 5000 rupees.

Based on the quality of food, I had assumed it was free.

Saisree said, 'How did you miss it? Didn't you see your friends paying the fee?'

That's when I realised I need a friend to know such things. I thought maybe I could ignore the rat infestation and patch things up with Nita. I invited Nita to have dinner with me at the mess.

At the mess, we settled down with our plates of mushy food when I asked her what the deal was with becoming a mess secretary.

'It is an easy way to make money,' Nita said. 'You get a bill from the vendor for twice as much as you spend on vegetables and grains. You split the profit with others. You'll see every mess secretary buying a new laptop or a two-wheeler at the end of the semester. You also get to dictate the menu, oversee cooking, and take the leftovers with you.'

It's so easy in the hostel, and probably anywhere, when you are part of a community. Like Saisree and her friends who can have each other's back, who help each other run scams, plagiarise, navigate the world of the hostel and their courses together. Saisree and I are in the same hostel, but we lead such different lives. Hers is one where she laughs all day with her friends and family as they cook together. Mine is of a sad queer who didn't pay her mess dues and is in deep financial trouble.

I feel a little bit envious.

14. Moving On

❁

I don't know how I'm going to pay the mess dues. I'd have budgeted for it if I had known I would have to pay mess dues. I had some leftover money last month, and I used it to buy two pairs of socks, two t-shirts, a meal from a nice restaurant, and the second cheapest bottle of Whisky. Now I have nothing left. I have two options: borrow money from someone or ask my mother for more money.

I could borrow, I have good credit-worthiness. I look like I have money based on the five-year-old macbook pro that I use. But I just don't know anyone who would have that much money to give me.

There is no other option; I have to ask my mother for more money.

Till now, I just lived with whatever she gave me. I made it work. Because I didn't ask her for more money, I felt okay to ignore her calls. Once I ignored her calls for a week and she texted me asking if I was okay or if I had been kidnapped by Naxalites. That's what she thinks of University of Hyderabad.

I didn't call my mother. I waited for her to call me. That was the only power I had left. When she did, we small-talked at first.

Then I said, 'I didn't know I had to pay mess dues. Three meals cost fifty a day for three months plus late fees. I need five thousand.'

She said the totally expected line, 'What about all the money I've already given you?'

My accounting knowledge came handy as I gave her a category-wise breakup of where all her money had gone. I was prepared for this so I wrote down arbitrary numbers on a piece of paper that I knew she would accept. All the money spent on liquor and cigarettes was disguised under scooter repairs.

'I don't have any money,' she said and proceeded to give a category-wise breakup of all her expenditure. A large proportion of her salary went to savings and if I ask her why she can't take money out of her savings for me, she'd again get into an entire spiel about how she is saving for retirement because she is sure I can't take care of her. So, I didn't go there.

'Well, I need this money. What do I do?' This is me telling her that I'm open to trade services for money.

'Are you coming to the anniversary celebrations that your father invited you to?' My mother said, trying to sound like it was a totally unrelated question. My parents have been 'together' for 25 years and they want to celebrate it grandly. They called it their 'Silver Jubilee'.

I had already RSVPd: Oh-hell-no.

But I need the money now, so she has leverage. I say, 'I'd love to come to your 25 years anniversary celebration!'

'Okay then. Let me see what I can do about the money,' she says before hanging up.

I got two pings on my phone. One from my bank telling me I got the money I asked for. Two, my flight ticket to Chennai where the anniversary celebrations were taking place in one week.

I paid my dues and flew to Chennai. I agreed to stay only for one night. Made up a story about mid-term tests in the university to get out sooner. Nobody cared, I guess they didn't want me to stay too long anyway.

The silver jubilee celebrations happened in a five-star restaurant. The moment we reached the venue, before we even got to our table, my parents wanted me to click pictures of them together. We spent over 20 minutes just taking pictures. Of my parents dressed in their best. Of the four of us, them, me, and my brother. Anybody could see from our smiling lips that we were one happy family.

We all got our own menus to order food. I read it three times and couldn't find a single thing I wanted to eat. Then I saw the prices. Every single item on the menu cost as much as my mess dues, the very reason I was there. My father started boasting about his successful relationship with my mother, telling me and my brother that we can never find love like the one they shared. Telling us that my mother was his mentor, as if he'd never beat her. I couldn't control myself, I started crying.

I cried because the meal cost so much more than I had spent on meals for three months, and I still wouldn't have a good meal. The hotel was so shiny and the waiters kept filling water in our glasses. I thought about my dingy room in the hostel where I was a few hours ago, and I wondered why even though the circumstances had changed so drastically, I still felt terrible.

I cried because Chennai's five-star hotels reminded me of a childhood memory. When I was three years old and my family lived in Chennai, my father didn't have the guts to tell his Brahmin parents that he drank alcohol. So he'd pretend he was a good father and husband spending time with his family and drag me and my mother to a five-star hotel every evening where we'd be forced to keep him company for three hours while he got sloshed. All the while my mother would smile-cry discreetly, whispering insults at him loud enough to only reach our ears.

When his business was not going well, we couldn't afford to go to a five-star hotel. Instead, my father would drive around the city drinking beer with us in the car. My mother would loudly cry, curse, and threaten to jump out of the moving car. I'd be stuck in the back seat at a time when they didn't have seatbelts or child seats. Every time my father lost control and slammed the car brakes, I'd fall head-first between the seats or slam my head on the radio dashboard when my father would quickly grab his beer bottle to save it from my head.

I cried because I was a sell-out. I was there to celebrate my parents' 25th anniversary when I hated their marriage more than anything. I hated all the trauma it had caused me. I remember when I was 10, I'd asked my mother why she wouldn't divorce my father. It was obvious even to me, a 10-year-old, that my mother was suffering abuse and should get a divorce. Of course it was obvious, everyone in my house, my grandparents included, felt terrible when my father got drunk every night and said nasty things to us. My grandmother and mother cried every night till their eyes dried out. My father tried to destroy our confidence, my brother's and mine, as much as he could. Yet, when I asked my mother why she wouldn't divorce him, she told me, a 10-year-old, that if she divorced my father, it would be hard to get me married 'into a good home'.

That broke me. I felt responsible for the misery for so many years. When I grew older, I realised that my mother had just told me a convenient lie that day, an easy explanation that would make her look like 'a good mother' who had sacrificed her happiness in favour of her child's future prospects. Sucks for her that I was 12 when I decided I was never going to get married. I didn't even know what sex was, but I knew I'd never get married. I wanted my mother's sacrifice (which I thought was the real reason she stayed with my father) to go to waste. To be worthless. Now I know she stayed with him for society's respect and financial security. Everything is always about fucking society and money.

I cried because I was still at my parent's mercy when I needed money. The book I was writing was a fantasy about a woman surviving on bare-minimum, a fantasy that would free me from the way my parents made me feel every time they waved their money in front of me. I want, more than anything else, to be independent enough to never see my parents again. The only way I can see that happening, given my issues, is if I somehow adjust to living in a poor neighbourhood and don't need much money. I know that can't happen because I'm pathetic.

As I cried, my father said, 'What's wrong with her?'

Like something was wrong with me and not them. Like they had nothing to do with whatever caused me to cry. Like I had spoiled the perfect evening of their perfect marriage with my silly emotions.

I went to the ladies' room and sobbed my eyes out. I came back to the table, ate nothing, and left.

*

Back in the hostel just an hour, and Saisree barged in again.

She had an interview for an internship. She was wearing an oversized blazer which I'm guessing belongs to her brother. She asked me if I could help her prepare for the interview.

'What questions will they ask?' she said. She really had no idea.

I spent the next hour telling her about different interview questions and the type of things she can and can't say.

'If I don't know English word, can I say in Telugu?' She asked.

'Ask the interviewer if being fluent in English is part of the job requirement. If yes, you have to answer in English. If not, and the interviewer knows Telugu, you can answer in Telugu,' I said.

'Okay.'

'They may ask who your role model is,' I said. 'Do you have a role model?'

'What is a role model?'

'Someone you admire, who you want to be like,' I said.

'My mother is my role model,'

'You have to explain a bit more when you answer,' I said. 'Why is she your role model?'

'She cooks and does everything for the family without complaining,' she said. 'I want to be like that'

'Oh, okay…'

'Is that a good answer?' she asked.

'Sure.'

After she left, I felt bad for not calling her out on her patronising 'mothers are self-sacrificial beings' comment. But at that moment, I thought maybe that's the answer most people would appreciate. Hell, if my mother was her interviewer, she'd love her for that answer. It shows that she upholds sentiments passed down by society without questioning them. A mind that has no questions has all the answers and won't break down every day. Okay, I'm being presumptuous.

But the conversation with Saisree also makes me think of my privilege. I don't even know how I learned to interview. I guess I learned it unconsciously from my upbringing or the private school I went to. Saisree and I might have the same degrees, she might even have a better GPA, but I'd always have a better chance at getting a job solely due to my privilege. I know how to interview, I can speak good enough English, and my Brahminical looks would certainly work the interviewers' bias in my favour.

I should be helping more people learn these skills so they'd have more options to choose from. But instead, I'm writing a book about a Brahmin girl adjusting to a poor neighbourhood? Is that a book anyone wants to read? How much more insensitive and tone-deaf can I be? No wonder everyone thinks the book is a comedy, it's a joke.

The biggest joke is the one scene of the novel that I've written so far. It's about how the protagonist realises that if she tried to rent a house in a slum, because she looks like a privileged Brahmin girl with her fair skin and well-groomed hair, her neighbours would assume that she was either an undercover police agent trying to bust illegal activities, or an anthropologist researcher writing a book about the poor, or a journalist doing a longform story on slum life. So she considers whether to introduce herself as a researcher or a journalist before having her neighbours assume the worst about her. I'm reading it now and wondering what it really means. Does it speak more to class and caste realities or the presumptuous Brahmin-ness of the protagonist and by extension, the author?

It makes me come to terms with how much I've embraced the performative aspects of my caste identity. How I emulate the aesthetics of a woman from a good family. It's in the way I dress, the way I move, the way I speak. It's why I dress so conservatively and can never even think of colouring my hair or getting a tattoo. It's in my polite etiquette, my good manners and my assiduous hiding of bad habits. It's almost the only thing I want strangers to perceive about me. My appearance screams out: Respect me, I'm a Brahmin.

It's true; I'd rather a stranger think I'm Brahmin than think I'm a lesbian. But why? Would I rather be seen as a Brahmin than a lesbian because men are excited by lesbians and the loose morals having a sexuality implies? Is it self-defence? I don't think so. My fencing teacher was a woman, and I let her say homophobic nonsense when there was no threat to me if I stopped her. Sexuality aside, I told Saisree I don't smoke or drink clearly to have her perceive me as a Brahmin girl from a good family when I had no reason to lie. How different am I from my father who hid his drinking habits from his parents? Or my mother who hid the abuse? I am my parents. They are just more outspoken and unapologetic about their prejudice and privilege, while I am more smug about being a better human being when I'm not.

Can I really not feel lust? Or am I just sexually repressed? I still can't admit to myself or anyone else that I enjoy having sex. I immediately feel so selfish just thinking about it. But how different is it from any other indulgence? Why don't I feel shame when I say I want to have a nice meal, but I feel it when I say I want to have a good time? Maybe because I want to perceive myself as pious and virtuous, even though I don't really believe there is something wrong with feeling lust. But I'm conditioned to respond that way, and I let myself be that way.

It's bloody convenient to be a Brahmin. It opens doors and people respect me for no reason. It's probably why I don't want to march for Rohith Vemula. Not because I am too busy to read about caste atrocities. It's not caste blindness, it's caste ignorance. I'd rather not engage in a narrative that makes out Brahmins as oppressors. I'd rather be unaware of the realities of caste discrimination. So I feel no shame or guilt from wanting to be perceived as a Brahmin.

I can't write a novel about a woman losing her privilege. It's stupid and tone deaf, and I also don't have the authenticity to write it. I cling to my Brahminical privilege, constantly benefit from it, without correcting or educating people what I really think of my caste. I dress conservatively and complain about everyone's hygiene based on the elitism of being born into a 'good family'.

My parents at least made money, what have I done? I keep telling myself that I want to live with fewer means to take the pressure off being 'conventionally' successful, but I can't go a day without whining about how difficult life is without material support for my disabilities and mental health issues. I am dreaming of being a writer, when my insecurities from dyslexia won't let me believe I can write a worthy sentence.

I keep enrolling in universities just to get stressed and drop out. I keep looking for love while I'm buried in the closet and hiding behind a convenient identity. I keep yearning for company just to speak lies to everyone I meet. I keep dreaming of independence while still getting sucked under my parent's shadow. I love being in impossible vicious circles where I can call myself a victim, but maybe I just really enjoy destroying myself.

But, honestly, what else can I do? I tried living as a starved Office Boy. I tried teaching myself skills and freelancing. I tried being honest and open. I tried coming out to everyone. I tried dealing with dyslexia. I tried writing. I tried. But I live in this world. A world where formal education is the only way to a legitimate career. A world where I could be suspended from the hostel for who I am. A world where I could flunk out of a university despite knowing all the answers just because I can't write them in the 'right' way or find questions confusing. A world where I can't even imagine what LGBTQ+ acceptance would look like. A world where I'm constantly stressed and restless. A world where nobody understands anything about me. A world where I don't feel safe.

Maybe I'm not pathetic. Maybe I'm just trying my best. Maybe I'm not a bad person. I'm so lonely; I have to defend myself to myself and protect myself from myself. Wish there was just one person in this world who knew me just enough to tell me when I need to be hard on myself and when I need to give myself a break. Won't that be great? If someone actually saw me for who I was? If someone understood me, or at least took some interest in me? If someone was kind to me and maybe even liked me a little? If someone would stop me right now and say: you are alright.

I am lying in this uncomfortable bed, alone in this dingy room. I feel sad that I haven't felt another person's warmth in a very long time, and I feel sad thinking I am unworthy of another person's warmth. I have been endlessly rambling to myself for the last few hours, and critically analysing my every thought, instinct, move. I feel like I am inside a ditch that I've dug—and I keep on digging, I keep tearing myself apart.

I don't feel safe alone anymore.

*

I've been spending a lot of time with a neighbour, Mridula. She moved into Gloria's room a few weeks ago. We met last week: I was throwing my trash in the wing's dustbin when I saw the infamous rat jump out of the bin and scurry away. Mridula, nearby, saw it and sighed.

'Do you know this one lives in my room's vent?' I asked.

'Nah, that one has a longer tail, this one is a different rat.' She went inside her room and came back with a sketchbook that had a sketch of the long-tailed rat that visits my vent—only the sketch looked as real as the rat itself, shadows and textures and all.

'Wow, you draw so well.'

'Had a figure study assignment and thought why not draw my nemesis,' she said, 'We should do something about that rat.' By 'we' she probably meant everyone in the wing, but the way she said 'we' sounded sweet.

'Do you want to help me kill it?' I asked.

We took my scooter to the supermarket and bought rat poison. The instructions said we should mix the poison with food. We didn't have any food with us.

'We probably shouldn't use food from the mess, no way a rat is going to eat that,' I said. She chuckled.

We finally mixed the poison with instant noodles. I helped her put heaps of the poisoned noodles in different spots in our wing and outside. We then made signs together that read: Rat poison in noodles! Don't eat! She was studying painting in the university; she doodled tiny rats eating noodles on the signs. I helped her tape the signs on the walls where we left the poison. We talked till late in the night about the pathetic hygiene of the hostel and our personal struggle with it.

Next morning, I saw four dead rats outside the hostel. The place was reeking of dead rats by noon when I was coming back from class. As I entered my wing, I saw Mridula telling the maid to scoop up the dead rats and throw them out. She smiled at me as I walked past her. She came to my room later and asked me if I wanted to have lunch with her.

She noticed that my door didn't fit inside the door's frame and asked, 'Do you want me to fix your door? I have sculpting tools, I can scrape the wood on your door and make it fit.'

'God, yes, thank you!'

She fixed my door, and we've been going to the mess hall together, having every meal together since.

Today I got an email that I'd been offered a place in a writing workshop where I'd be mentored by South-Asian-origin authors from the UK. I'd get to workshop two short stories—been thinking of story ideas all morning. I feel like writing stories about what it means to be queer in India; I think I might have a nuanced perspective on it.

It is a quiet evening in the hostel, the monsoon breeze blowing into my room through the open windows. I've spent the day at my desk, typing on my laptop, drafting my first queer short story while Mridula sat on my bed, embroidering a cross-stitch design of two women drinking tea.

My life changed the day I met Mridula. I did not know it then, but in a few days Mridula would start sleeping in my room, and in a few weeks we'd kiss. In two years, I'd graduate at the top of my class and be awarded a gold medal, and Section 377 would be read down. In four years, Mridula and I would buy a three-bedroom house together in Hyderabad and finally, in a home of my own, I'd find the courage to dust off this notebook and write it into a book.